VIDAL IN VENICE

GORE VIDAL

VIDAL IN VENICE

EDITED BY
George Armstrong

PHOTOGRAPHS BY
TORE GILL

SEE P. 33

SUMMIT BOOKS
IN ASSOCIATION WITH ANTELOPE

The Lion's Mouth, or 'denunciation box', in the Doge's Palace.
It is still open to suggestions, but only from Venetians.
The inscription particularly urges squealing on citizens
who do not report their full incomes.

This SUMMIT BOOKS edition, 1987
First published in the United States in 1985 by
SUMMIT BOOKS,
a Division of Simon & Schuster, Inc.
Simon & Schuster Building
Rockefeller Center
1230 Avenue of the Americas, New York, NY 10020
SUMMIT BOOKS and colophon are trade marks of Simon & Schuster, Inc.

First published in Great Britain in 1985 by
George Weidenfeld & Nicolson Limited

Printed in Italy

10 9 8 7 6 5 4 3 2 1

Library of Congress Cataloging-in-Publication Data

Vidal, Gore, 1925–
Vidal in Venice.

Bibliography: p.
Includes index.

1. Venice (Italy)—Description—1981–
2. Vidal, Gore, 1925–   —Journeys—Italy—Venice.
3. Authors, American—20th century—Journeys—Italy—
Venice.   I. Armstrong, George   II. Gill, Tore.
III. Title.

DG674.2.V44   1987   914.5′31   87–6498

ISBN 0–671–60691–3
ISBN 0–671–64536–6 (pbk.)

CONTENTS

The Grand Canal.
Gore Vidal seated in a gondola.

PREFACE

IN my youth, it seemed that every American had an Aunt Fenita. No matter where one's family lived or was from, Aunt Fenita was always from Ohio. As she grew older, she tended to move east to New York State or Connecticut, where she would settle in a white-frame house in a town with a name like Plandome. By definition, Aunt Fenita was of a certain age, as the French say; and, widow or spinster, she lived contentedly alone. She had enough money to travel, and that is what she did best – and most. Since European travel was still an adventure for Americans before World War II, Aunt Fenita was positively glamorous in her knowledge of steamship lines and railroad schedules, hotels and *pensions*. She was what was then called a globe-trotter. Had anyone collected her postcards, he would have had a panoramic, even Braudelesque, view of just what it was that our innocents abroad most liked to look at: in Aunt Fenita's case, the Matterhorn loomed rather larger than the Louvre; but then she never saw an alp that she didn't like. Of course, we were Alpine folk.

Aunt Fenita was the self-appointed emissary between the family in America and the family in Europe. Before World War II, we were remarkable in that the European branch was far more distinguished than the American. Things had not gone well for the first two generations in God's country. But in Europe, titles abounded; and though she always got them wrong, Aunt Fenita was an eager, even obsessed, genealogist. Postcards of castles where relatives lived, or allegedly lived, would arrive, such as Schloss Heidegg in Gelfingen. A neatly-drawn arrow, pointing to a noble casement, marks 'Your grandmother Caroline's room'. On Aunt Fenita's death, trunks were found filled with Brownie snapshots of houses, castles, stout ladies, bearded burghers, coats-of-arms, pressed flowers from gardens of relatives in Feldkirch, St. Gallen, Unterwalden, Lucerne, and a list of the doges of Venice – her greatest discovery and the family's Rosetta Stone – of whom three were called Vidal or Vitale, the magic name triply underlined in Aunt Fenita's triumphant porphyry-purple ink. There were also postcard views of, variously, the church, the piazza and the Rio S. Vidal.

I was much impressed; and grateful to Aunt Fenita for connecting me with that slightly comic title of doge ('Git along little dogie' was a popular old

Western song). Of course one never took Aunt Fenita all that seriously; even so, there was something mesmerising about her – the grey knowing eyes, framed by steel-rimmed pince-nez; the huge dentures not unlike those of Woodrow Wilson; and, always, the knowledge that she had been to Europe a thousand times, and met Cousin Ludwig, Cousin Emma and all those mysterious von Hartmanns and von Baldeggs and de (why not 'von'?) Traxlers. The family was mittel mittel-europa in spades, occupying that area which was once the Roman province of Rhaetia, an Alpine district which Tiberius filled with legionnaires as a defence against the German tribes. At Aquileia, I have worshipped at a monument to a defunct Roman army officer named Vitalis; his descendants are everywhere in that part of the world and, literally, lively.

Rhaetia has now been split up by three countries: Switzerland, Austria and Italy. Our family lived – and lives – in all three sections, as if the province was still a living entity. There is even a Rhaetian language, Romansch, now spoken by very few people; rich in triple dipthongs, it is close to the vulgar Latin of two millennia ago.

Inspired no doubt by the restless ghost of Aunt Fenita, I finally went to the back, as it were, of all those postcards. I drove from Zürich to Liechtenstein to nearby Feldkirch in the Austrian Vorarlberg. Here, from 1300 to 1848, the Vidals were apothecaries – more like wholesale chemists – and Vidalhaus still stands, a splendid fourteenth-century arcaded building, currently occupied by the provincial tax office. The setting is best described not by me but by that wicked travel writer of genius, Norman Douglas, who was brought up near Feldkirch, and who describes the wild countryside in a book due for revival, *Together*.

By the nineteenth century, the Vidals were renting out flats in Vidalhaus, and one was home to the late good President Frei of Chile. Were there any Vidals left? The priest at St. Stefan's Church thought not. Together we went through the registry of births. There was my great-grandfather Eugen Fidel Vidal, born in 1820; but after him, the line ends. I know little about him. He graduated from the University of Lausanne; he married Emma, an heiress from Lucerne (who was promptly and permanently disinherited); he arrived in Wisconsin in 1848. No matter what he put his hand to, he failed. Then, one day, he disappeared. The bitter Lucerne heiress supported their four children by translating French, German and Italian stories into English for newspapers. After a twenty-year absence, Eugen Fidel came home. Emma committed him to the poorhouse, where, each evening, he put on a tattered red velvet smoking jacket; he died a long way from Vidalhaus.

As the priest and I went through the records, I noticed that the family vanished at the end of the sixteenth century; then they surfaced again in the

*Rio de S. Vidal,
the small canal which
passes behind the Church
of S. Vidal, carrying its
share of rubbish out to the
Grand Canal.*

1790s, when one Johan Felix Vidal reappeared in Feldkirch, reoccupied Vidalhaus and married the daughter of the burgher-meister, who gave birth to the poorhouse-bound Eugen Fidel Vidal. Where, I asked the priest, was the family from 1590 to 1970? Friuli, he said, pointing to the yellowed page. Johan Felix was born in the Friuli, at Forni à Voltri. And where – or what – I asked, in Fenitaesque confusion, is Friuli? A part of Rhaetia that is now a part of Italy and, before that, for centuries, a province of Venice. I knew ecstasy! *The Vidals had gone south to be doges.* Aunt Fenita was vindicated. Git along, little dogie, indeed. Had we not, in Byzantine splendour, thrice wed the sea?

In due course, I visited the mountain town of Forni à Voltri. The church records were missing for births and deaths; but the marriage records were intact. We were still apothecaries; but a large number had become priests. In the high main street, circled by sharp alps, I stopped an old man to ask him the way to the cemetery. When he looked me directly in the eye, I found myself staring into my dead father's agate-yellow eyes. But then, as it turned out, everyone in the village looked like my family, except for the kindly Virgilian ghost of Aunt Fenita. She was not Romanischer but Ulster, and shared with us the turbulent blood of that most dear of presidents, William McKinley. She

*A Vidale family
gravestone in the Friuli,
the region north of Venice.*

was also very good about the fact that our family had been Roman Catholic, something so unfashionable at the turn of the century that Emma, after a losing battle with the Jesuit order over some property in Feldkirch, became an atheist, that is, an Episcopalian.

The town baker is called Michele Vidali. I told him that I was sad to see that a vowel had been added to the name. He said it was inevitable now that Friuli was neither Venetian nor Austrian but Italian. I introduced him to my uncle, a retired air force general. To make conversation, the general, Felix (yet again!) Vidal, said that he had been based in Italy during the war, and that he had led several bombing expeditions over Germany. Michele looked grim. 'Yes,' he said, 'I remember. Your flight path was just there, to the west.' He pointed to an attractive alp. 'You bombed Innsbruck, didn't you?' The general said that he had. Michele sighed; then he produced a bottle of grappa, and we drank to Vidals with and without vowels at the end of their names. I daresay had Michele and not Felix gone to West Point, Michele would have bombed Innsbruck.

I came to Venice late. The city has been so over-praised that I saw no reason for visiting what I had already heard too much about. Why fall in love with that glorious light which Canaletto and Bellotti and Guardi have dealt with so much better than the retinas of my myopic eyes could ever do? Also, pre- and post-war Venice was a centre of what used to be called café society, and I steered clear of all that. The thought of Oswald Mosley romping in the sand of the Lido was my idea of true death in Venice. But, in due course, at some point in the 1960s, I came to Venice; checked into the Danieli Hotel; escorted the beautiful Clare Boothe Luce to a ball held in the Palazzo Rezzonico. We arrived by boat, as torches flared in rooms where once the Brownings had flared or flickered. Paparazzi cameras recorded our arrival. A string orchestra played Offenbach while cloudy Venetian mirrors reflected crystal chandeliers, diamonds, and every splendid familiar face that one had spent a lifetime avoiding, including (could it be?) Oswald Mosley's. One had stepped into the pages of a novel by Frances Parkinson Keyes, Aunt Fenita's favourite cicerone to Romance. And so it came to pass that at a green damask-covered table, where Browning had worked beneath a huge, gaudy, candy-like Venetian chandelier, beautiful Clare and I got into one hell of a political row. But that was in another country; and besides, she still is fair.

Every year I come to Venice at least once, in August, because a friend is only free in that month and she loves Venice. I hate the place in August (too many people, and the heat is African), but the air-conditioning at the Gritti is excellent, which it should be as one is paying for what seems to be the mineral rights to Antarctica; and there are still those churches to see and see again, and the islands of the lagoon to explore. I particularly like Burano, a miniature city on whose church wall there is a plaque commemorating those who died in World War I: three Vidals. There is also a plaque to those who fell in World War II: not one Vidal is listed – lesson learned. As for our three doges, Aunt Fenita, alas, got it all wrong, as usual. The *first* name of three doges was Vidal. So that little dogie has finally got along; nor were we to be found in the Book of Gold where the noble families are listed. On the other hand, we are well and truly represented in the Venetian telephone directory and Vidal Soap – the Lifebuoy of Italy – seems rather more our speed. Six centuries of pharmaceuticals, concentrated in a cake of soap. (You can smell the *pine*!)

For some years now I have spent New Year in Venice. That is the magic time. The weather is apt to be good while the light – oh, that light! – is nacreous, for once a proper use of that word. There are few foreigners on view, and Harry's Bar is more than ever a shrine to the martini while the light. . . . But I've just done the light.

There is nothing quite like writing and appearing in a two-hour television documentary on Venice to stumble on a truth: as, talking and talking, I slowly sank into a mud flat near Torcello, I realized that not only did I have nothing to say but there *is* nothing to say. The place is there – still. Look at it. In a world of glass and plastic, of toxic wastes and poisonous air and lethal rain, Venice is as scarred and damaged as everything else. But, even so, the city in the sea still remains like some natural – that is, currently, *in*human – formation created out of a sense of wholeness that we have entirely lost as the second Christian millennium sputters (you pick your own verb) to its unmourned end.

I

THE FACE OF VENICE

It has been said more than once that the Square of St. Mark's is
— now brace yourself for our first cliché —
the drawing room of Europe. And indeed it is, but then
Venice itself is perhaps the most beautiful cliché on earth.

VENICE is best seen at its emptiest, at dawn, before the tourists arrive on the scene. For the Square of St. Mark's, a symbol of the city, is all too often the most crowded, although always the most beautiful, of Europe's many drawing rooms, both indoor and outdoor. The first-time visitor to Venice may make a bee-line for a chair in that marble-colonnaded parlour. But the frequent visitor knows better – and may avoid St. Mark's altogether. That takes considerable strategy, but it can be done. The trouble with Venice is that all movement is either by foot or by boat, and all foot navigation ultimately leads you to a bridge where you are forced to converge with other walkers. Venice is a labyrinth which is difficult to master. It also seems to have been designed in such a way that, however much you try, you are helplessly funnelled into one of the main streets leading to St. Mark's. It is an astounding fact that no map exists which both shows and names each Venetian street. So the traveller who boasts that he can study the map, leave it at the hotel, and get to where he wants to go is out of luck in Venice. Wherever he may be heading, he is bound to end up in St. Mark's Square.

The majority of tourists anywhere in Italy are Italians, and even though you may not be aware of this, the Venetians certainly are. Most Italian tourists are day-trippers – families, parishioners led by their priest, entire classrooms of rowdy schoolchildren happy to be anywhere but in school. But there are also hordes of Bavarian peasants, who *do* arrive at dawn in their hired bus, toting their lunch of sausages, brown bread, and wine in string-bags, and who return to their farms the following dawn. After writing some postcards, and maybe buying a gondola-shaped ashtray, all that these day-trippers leave behind them are a few lire and a lot of rubbish.

There has been a ten-year debate in the city council about limiting the number of tourists who may enter Venice during the high season. Even

Gondolas moored along the Riva degli Schiavoni at
sunrise. The domes of S. Maria della Salute are just
visible in the distance, together with the Palladian
Church of the Zitelle on the island of the Giudecca.
On the right is the Piazzetta with its two columns
topped by the Lion of St. Mark and St. Todaro, and
behind them Sansovino's Library, the Biblioteca Marciana
*(*marciana *is the adjectival form of 'St. Mark's'),*
which was originally Venice's Mint.

ABOVE The campanile, or bell-tower, of St. Mark's Square. The original bell-tower, completed under Doge Vidale Michiel II in the twelfth century, collapsed in an accordion-like heap on 14 July 1902, a few minutes before 10 am, with no casualties.

LEFT St. Mark's Square. Venice has been called 'the place where lions fly and pigeons walk', but something or someone has alarmed these fattened birds enough to get them momentarily aloft. It could have been the Grim Reaper as, according to a folk tale, the Square's pigeons only take wing and fly to the mainland (probably into a farmer's oven) when they know their time is up.

*There is no sight more
beautiful than Venice
under a snowfall. History
records an event even
rarer: the Grand Canal
freezing, and Venetians
celebrating by roasting pigs
in the middle of the lagoon.*

though the closure of the causeway that connects Venice with the mainland is easy enough – it was done during the last days of Carnival in 1984–85, when the number of revellers in St. Mark's Square was estimated to exceed 100,000 people – a 'democratic' filtering system for tourists during the rest of the year has yet to be devised.

Venice should also be seen in winter, a winter dawn if you like, for under a heavy snowfall it is the most beautiful sight on earth. But beware. If the snow freezes, the bridges, which are really flights of steps, become hazardous. Winter is the only season in which Venice is both visible and sometimes also invisible, for from November to mid-March there are very few tourists. The rest of the year they 'swarm like locusts' as a Venice city councillor put it, St. Mark's, the Rialto and the Accademia being the three bases that everyone feels they must touch before making the home-run.

Venice is like a once-great beauty who deserves to be seen by candlelight, and the soft light of winter works like a photographer's air-brush on the city's many cracks and wrinkles. Venice is particularly beautiful in a winter mist. But only for one day, and not in those frequent dense fogs when even the *vaporetti* (water-buses) cannot safely navigate the Grand Canal.

In winter, too, there is a real chance of being hindered by the *acqua alta* (high water), which happens about fifty-five times a year. The approach of these high tidal waters, which cover the city's lower areas (St. Mark's being one) with two or three feet of water, is announced in the morning newspapers. If the water is expected to be exceptionally high, sixteen exceptionally loud and alarming sirens warn Venetian merchants to put their merchandise on the highest shelf. But the lagoon's tidal waters follow the laws of the universe (or of the moon?) and reverse themselves every six hours. Even the *acqua alta* can be considered part of 'seeing' Venice and the Venetians.

The clichés about Venice are imposed upon us because, like most clichés, they are based on true observations which have occurred to some of the greatest and most modest minds alike. 'Venice is unique' is the supreme, mother-cliché of them all. And no other three words can ever be truer. 'There is nothing new to be said about her [Venice] certainly . . . it would be a sad day indeed where there should be something new to say', wrote Henry James a hundred years ago. 'Nothing can be said here (*including this statement*) that has not been said before', wrote Mary McCarthy, many years later in *Venice Observed*. When you go to Venice for the first time, *unlace* yourselves for your own clichés.

ABOVE High water, which occurs when an exceptionally high tide from the Adriatic is carried into the lagoon by strong winds, is no longer unusual but, rather, routine. Damage to buildings, houses and shops is enormous. Political parties dither over projects presented by panels of experts to reduce the frequency of the acqua alta. In Venice, this is called 'passing the bucket'.

RIGHT The private face of Venice: reflections in one of the city's smaller canals, the Ramo de l'Agnella.

II

IN THE BEGINNING

In all of history, there have been only three million Venetians.
This is an amazing statistic, considering that this small city on a
group of islands in a lagoon at the northern end of the Adriatic Sea
was once the head of a great maritime empire – an empire
that produced Bellini and Vivaldi as well as
Marco Polo and Casanova.

THIS unlikely, watery city. Where did it start? Venice emerged, like life itself, from the mud. The mud of a large lagoon to which mainlanders had come for centuries to fish, to pan for salt. But no one thought of building a city until the Roman Empire began to fall apart in the fifth century AD. A thousand barbarian tribes were on the move. From the German forests, from the plains of Asia they came – Goths, Huns and Lombards. The Roman cities of the mainland were sacked and burned, their populations massacred. The survivors, anti-gothic to the core, took to their boats and moved their families and their sheep to the islands, seeking the safety of a vast moat to protect them from the enemy, who were not good seamen. Here they were secure. They were also surprisingly successful. Not only were they able to ignore the advances of Attila the Hun (who, as an equestrian, was probably less than charmed by Venetian mud), but they also cornered the salt trade. Men cannot live without salt. Today the world is amazed by the wealth that oil has brought to Arab deserts. But a thousand years ago, the world was equally bemused by the fact that the original Venetians had been able to make such a fortune out of their muddy lagoon – with salt.

Some one thousand, five hundred and sixty-three years ago – on 15 March we are told – a city was founded on one of these islands. At least that is the legend. Anyone wishing to understand the history of early Venice must start with Torcello, and we know for certain that Torcello – a miniature city with a miniature cathedral – was well established by the seventh century, and quickly became an important trading centre. Initially it would seem to have had a population of about one hundred, many of whom were from the mainland

LEFT Silted mud from mainland rivers created the islets which were to become Venice – a world capital built of granite and marble, supported by many millions of wooden pilings.

The Church of S. Fosca on the island of Torcello with the bell-tower of the cathedral on the left. This beautiful complex of buildings and a few ruins are all that remain of this city of a thousand inhabitants to which the first refugees came in the seventh century before they founded Venice.

A broken statue of Aphrodite, decorating a pathway near Torcello's small museum.

RIGHT
Torcello Cathedral: its Venetian-byzantine mosaics, depicting The Last Judgement, date from the twelfth and thirteenth centuries. Torcello was a bishop's see, older and once richer than Venice itself. But malaria and migration to Venice over the last thousand years has left the island with a population of just one hundred.

VIRGO DINATVMPRECE PVLSA TERGER·

·MHP· ·ΘV·

An aerial view of Venice from the south by the seventeenth-century Bavarian artist, Josef Heinz. The Bucintoro can be seen in the basin of St. Mark's surrounded by an armada of Venetian galleys and black gondolas.

city of Altinum, or Heraclea (aerial photographs have recently uncovered the ruins of this ancient city lying beneath cultivated ricefields on the mainland). The presence of a cathedral would suggest that this refugee colony, which eventually numbered 20,000 (now reduced to one hundred again), prospered. The influence of Byzantium still lives in the mosaics of the cathedral (recently restored through Britain's Venice in Peril Fund in collaboration with American and Italian groups), where Christ Pantocrater surveys heaven and hell, where the Mother of God descends from the shadowless gold of eternity. (Oh, how prettily one is obliged to soliloquise on television!)

In the year 810, Pepin, son of Charlemagne, conquered the mainland. But when he tried to invade the islands of the lagoon, the islanders united and stopped him, though he did succeed in conquering the islet of Malamocco. James Morris in *Venice* tells the story not only wonderfully well, but creates a brand new 'legend':

Only one old woman, so the story goes, had stayed behind in Malamocco, determined to do or die, and this patriotic crone was summoned to the royal presence. 'Which is the way to Rivo Alto?' demanded Pepin, and the old lady knew her moment had come. Quavering was her finger as she pointed across the treacherous flats, where the tide swirled deceitfully, and the mud oozed, and the seaweed swayed in turbulence. Tremulous was her voice as she answered the prince. 'Sempre diritto', she said; and Pepin's fleet, instantly running aground, was ambushed by the Venetians and utterly humiliated.

It was to the increased safety of the Rivo Alto, or Rialto, which means 'high embankment', that some of Torcello's inhabitants moved after Pepin's invasion. That was the beginning of Venice, an outpost for 'mighty, downtown' Torcello. Created from the silt brought down from mainland rivers, the Venice that we know, like the Venice that the world has known for 1,100 years, still stands on those small islands of the Rialto. Much of the city is man-made – the original Venetians were constantly filling in and enlarging this cluster of islets through which runs a river, now known as the Grand Canal, formed in the shape of an 'S' as reflected in a mirror. If the Venetians had arranged – as they could have done – for their river to flow in a straight course, like the Hudson, visitors to Venice would get lost less often than they do. When you are lost in Venice and ask for directions, the answer today is still '*sempre diritto*', or 'straight ahead'. The information is always correct – unless pursued to its limits, a watery canal. The city's signposts are equally helpful. In Campo S. Salvador there are, side by side, two signs directing you to the railway station. One points to the left, the other to the right. *Sempre diritto* would have done as well.

Venice began to establish itself. It now had the only elected leader in the

The Giving of the Ring to the Doge
by Paris Bordone, c.1533.
Painted for the Scuola of
St. Mark's, this painting
depicts a fisherman who,
trembling, ascends the steps
of the throne to bring the
Doge the golden ring.

During the ancient Wedding of the Sea ceremony, the doge would be rowed out in state into the Adriatic where he would toss a gold ring into the sea, and declare that Venice had taken the Adriatic as its bride.

world other than the pope – the Most Serene Prince, the Doge of Venice. The doge was a gilded icon, whose most splendid moment occurred on Ascension Day when he went forth in splendour on his barge, and threw a gold wedding ring into the sea with the words: 'We wed you O sea, as a sign of true and perpetual dominion'. As marriage vows go, this one would fit well Petrucchio, the Shakespearean hero who thought that he had tamed Catherine, the shrew. As time has shown, with two devastating floods in the last twenty years, and with the submerged stone foundations of the great palaces so eroded that, during a 1985 inspection by frogmen, 'they looked like Swiss Cheese', the sea is far from being dominated. Although more can be done to hold it back, one day the sea is going to reclaim the two and a half square miles which Venetians have occupied, almost against nature.

This dogal ceremony, which the mayor of Venice revised in 1978 (pomp supplied by the Italian navy) began in the year 1177, when the Venetians negotiated a peace pact between two greedy powers – the papacy and the

Today, the Venetian mayor, suitably costumed, is rowed out to sea to repeat the ceremony, but the gold ring has been replaced by a floral wreath.

If this painting by the nineteenth-century English artist John Bunney, entitled The West Front of St. Mark's, *is faithful, what we see today is a much-faded image.*
St. Mark's was modelled on Constantinople's Church of the Holy Apostles. Historians in the past have referred to the building as being Byzantine-gothic in style, but forty years ago Bernard Berenson revisited the church and declared it to be completely Byzantine, albeit Venetian-style.
To Mark Twain, it looked like 'a warty bug, out for a stroll'. Ruskin said that it was a church you could pass without ever looking up; the façade is certainly best seen, and indeed only seen, from the distance Bunney chose.

As depicted in the mosaics of St. Mark's Church, the body of St. Mark was smuggled into Venice from Alexandria in 829.

The saint's stolen body was packed into a casket of pork. The customs officials at Alexandria, being Moslem, were repulsed by the casket's contents, and the saint passed through to his new destination unnoticed. He was acclaimed saint-protector of Venice, and the evangelist's name, along with the bronze lion which the Venetians also adopted, became a symbol of the city's strength and independence from the rest of Europe.

Germanic Holy Roman Empire. The Emperor, Frederick Redbeard, was the loser of that round; the Doge, Sebastiano Ziani, required him to kiss Pope Alexander's foot and then, in front of St. Mark's Church, to help His Holiness mount the Papal mule. The Pope rewarded the Doge with a golden ring, a copy of which was tossed into the sea on Venice's annual wedding day. The ring, of course, was recovered, either by divers or by a strong thread which was attached to it. Waste not, want not, as the Venetians do not say but do. Today, the mayor offers the sea a floral wreath.

The ceremony was recognition of Venice's authority and dominion over the Adriatic. The Republic had achieved political independence from the mainland and was transformed into a sovereign state, soon to become one of the great powers.

Every major city in Christendom had its patron saint. Usually, he was a local, whose life had been exemplary, whose death had been grisly, whose earthly remains could heal and sanctify. Unfortunately the Venetians had been much too busy with worldly matters to produce a first-class saint of their very own. So, in due course, they stole one. And not only one. Two Venetian buccaneers, in 829, stole the bones of St. Mark the Evangelist from his tomb at Alexandria. The enterprising thieves were able to smuggle their contraband saint in a casket labelled 'pork' (pork being forbidden to Moslems). When the thieves arrived in Venice they were given a heroes' welcome, and the bones were placed in the Doge's private chapel, which was re-named for the saint. Less than a century later, the chapel was destroyed by fire and no trace of the bones could be found. After a number of saintless years, a seance with the Holy Ghost was arranged and, right on cue, the stones of one of the chapel's pillars began to split, and the bones, one by one, reappeared.

The Church of S. Rocco, and the *scuola* next door (*scuola* means guild, or trade union, hall), were built to honour France's St. Roch, whose remains were stolen from Montpelier by Venetian 'pilgrims' to his shrine. This particular theft was for medical or hygienic reasons, however, since it was thought that St. Roch could ward off plagues. St. Mark's Church, which became Venice's cathedral in the nineteenth century, also contains a knife used to cut bread at the Last Supper, a finger of Mary Magdalene, the stone on which John the Baptist was beheaded, as well as one of John's four authenticated skulls, and one of St. George's numerous arms – perhaps the very one that he used to slay the dragon. On the island of Murano, the Church of S. Donato outdoes St. Mark's. It has the bones of the kindly *dragon* which that fierce S. Donato martyred.

If the Church of St. Mark's looks odd to western eyes it is for a very good reason. It is *eastern*. It is Byzantine. Why did the Venetians – who were western and Roman – decide to build something that was eastern and Greek? It started with the Fourth Crusade, when the power and the glory began.

III
THE BIRTH OF AN EMPIRE

For a thousand years Venice survived as an independent republic.
The Most Serene Republic, they called themselves —
somewhat optimistically, because the history of Venice
was actually a stormy one.

Venice is still called 'La Serenissima' today in the Italian press, and you might well think the name comes from the absence of automobiles and the relative silence. It was instead a title bestowed upon the city by a pope during one of those rare periods when Venice and the papacy were not at war with each other. For much of the Republic's 1,100 years of independence and power were spent warring, plotting wars, profiteering from other nations' wars – and serenely counting the loot brought them by wars.

A city the size of New York's Central Park was to overwhelm Constantinople, the greatest and richest city on earth; to acquire Crete, the islands of the Cyclades, and the Peloponnese. By 1400 Venice controlled Corfu, the base at Nauplia, and the coast of Dalmatia. By 1500 it was the largest empire in the West. And the Arsenal was its heart. For the first time

Vittore Carpaccio's The Lion of St. Mark, *dated 1516. The winged lion is found all over Venice, but nowhere is the original portrayed better than by Carpaccio. This lion seems to have put his paw on foreign soil that the Venetians have just conquered. The Doge's Palace, where this picture hangs, forms the backdrop. The State barge is moored alongside the waterfront, while the ships emerging from the Arsenal on the right allude to Venetian dominion of the seas.*

The Arsenal. First built in 1104, this shipyard was an industrial complex employing over 16,000 workers. Its modern, assembly-line techniques could turn out one completely outfitted galley in a single day. The word 'Arsenal' was a Venetian invention, being a corrupted form of darsina'a, the Arabic word for 'house of industry'. Dante is known to have visited the Arsenal, and its vats of boiling pitch, used to caulk the galleys, inspired him to one of his darkest images in the Inferno. Though protected by natural moats – the sea and the lagoon – Venice was the only major power without a fortress, so the first major building to be fortified was the essential shipyard. Later, the foundries in the Jewish ghetto area were moved to the Arsenal, which was constantly being enlarged until the Republic capitulated to Napoleon.

anywhere on earth, ships were turned out by mass production. When the Arsenal was at its peak, 16,000 craftsmen could turn out an entire fighting galley in a single day. But then 'arsenal' comes from the Arab word which means 'house of industry'. So at the core of this impregnable city in the lagoon's centre was this impregnable arsenal and anchorage. From here half the Mediterranean was to fall, in due course, to the Lion of Venice. Sea and ships, energy and cunning, buying and selling and then – Empire.

The lions which guard the Arsenal come from all over the world. In fact, no lion was safe if a Venetian was in the neighbourhood. But then the lion, which had been the emblem of St. Mark, was now the symbol of Venice and its empire: a winged lion with an open bible, displaying the text 'Peace be unto thee, Mark'. The lion over the Arsenal door has prudently shut his copy of the Gospel, no doubt on the grounds that it would be too hypocritical to speak of peace at the entry to the world's biggest and busiest military shipyard and cannon foundry. The other two lions by the entrance were collected by Doge Francesco Morosini, best known for blowing the lid off the Athens Parthenon because the Turks were using the ancient temple to store gunpowder. The seated lion once guarded the port of Piraeus. In the last century it was discovered that the curious scratch marks on its flanks were not due to the ill-grooming of the sculptor's model, but to Scandinavian mercenaries, brought in to put down a tax rebellion in Athens in 1040. If you believe this story, and can *find* the Norse graffiti, you merit a translation: 'Haakon, together with Ulf, Asmund, and Worn, conquered this port'. The first named got home in time to become, the same year, King of Norway. Twenty-six years later, he was killed at Stamford Bridge in Yorkshire, his luck having run out. The lion he defaced had, all in all, better luck and is today in a setting more majestic and imposing than any place in Piraeus. And *Pax Tibi Melina Mercouri*, too.

Whenever life started to get boring at home, the leaders of the West would call for a Crusade against the Moslems. Why? Because they – the Infidels – controlled the Holy Land. The Venetians sat out the first three Crusades, but joined the fourth for a lot of money. A line in Byron's *Childe Harold*, most of which was written in Venice, reads 'O, for one hour of blind, old Dandolo!' and one knows what Byron meant. Enrico Dandolo was the doge who led the Venetians on the Fourth Crusade in 1204, when he was allegedly ninety-seven and blind. Though the purpose of the expedition was to free the Holy Land from the Infidels, Dandolo arranged for the fleet to stop off en route and seize Constantinople, directing the barrage of 'fire bombs' himself and being the first to spring ashore. Then the Venetians sacked that most Christian city of Constantine. Furiously, the Pope denounced the Venetians, who serenely replied: 'We are Venetians first, Christians second.' It may someday turn out that Dandolo was really only eighty-two, and with failing eyesight, but that

This lion paws no book but carries on his person a literate message. He once stood guard over Porto Lion – today's Piraeus – probably named after him, and was brought to Venice as booty. Scratches on his chest, flanks and back were deciphered in the nineteenth century as eleventh-century advertising in Norse.

would not detract from his leadership and courage. For it took courage for a fleet of Venetian galleys, sailing off on a Christian mission, one blessed by the Pope, to surprise, attack and seize another great *Christian* city. It was, of course, good for business – every pair of palms in the Rialto must have rubbed together when the news reached Venice, in anticipation of new cartels in Venetian imports and exports.

Most of Venice's stolen relics and ancient art objects were seized during wars or the Crusades. Plainly, their galleys never needed ballast for the return voyage. The loot was so great that much of it stayed for years on the waterfront, awaiting suitable distribution. The famous horses of St. Mark's were spoils brought home from the sacking of Constantinople.

As sea lords go, the Venetians were surprisingly good landlords. They tried to do things by diplomacy. Since it was expensive to maintain armies in hostile countries, the Venetians often left the administration of their possessions to the locals. They themselves maintained ports, trading posts and an occasional

VICTORIÆ NAVALIS MONIMENTVM · M · D · L · XXI ·

This is probably the youngest winged lion in Venice, carved to decorate the land-gate to the Arsenal, which was the work of Antonio Gambello – and in 1460 the first architectural signal that the Florentine Renaissance style had reached Venice. The lion holds his Bible shut. The usual inscription, 'Peace be unto thee, Mark my Evangelist', would not have seemed appropriate over the door of a building dedicated to making cannons and warships. The Latin inscription refers to Venice's great naval victory over the Turks at Lepanto in 1571.

St. Mark's lion travelled wherever Venice ruled, and here adorns a fort at Heraklion, Crete.

LEFT *The look-out post of a Venetian fortress at Rethimnon, Crete.*

The islands of the Cyclades were part of the loot from the Fourth Crusade. They were governed by Marco Sanudo, who settled the islands with his friends and relations whose coats-of-arms can still be seen over doorways on Naxos.

fortress. The islands of the Cyclades were part of the loot from the Fourth Crusade, which the Venetians then turned over to a young nobleman, Marco Sanudo, nephew of blind old Dandolo. He ruled over these seventeen beautiful islands as the Venetian Duke of Naxos. Naxos is now a popular resort in the Aegean. But you can still see the fortified town that Sanudo built over 750 years ago. He settled Naxos and the other islands with his friends and relations, and their coats-of-arms are still to be found over doorways, and the ruins of his castle still remain. The masonry is held together with pink mortar from the island of Santorini, mixed with egg yolks. The result is harder than stone, and a minatory monument to high cholesterol. Although Naxos is now entirely Greek and its religion Orthodox, there is still a Roman Catholic cathedral and there are still many families of Venetian ancestry. All in all, the Venetians were not oppressive rulers in the Cyclades. Since they were there to protect trade routes, each island was not so much a territory of any great value as a sort of stationary ship, to be of use in the servicing of the Venetian fleet.

But when Venice came to conquer the vast island of Crete, the Republic behaved with uncharacteristic stupidity. Since there were ten times as many highly bad-tempered, patriotic Cretans as there were Venetians in all of Venice, Crete was an ideal place for the invaders to mind their own business, which was business, and let the Cretans govern themselves. But Crete was too important for the Venetians. They needed grain, wine and oil. So they settled a number of their noble families on the island, which they then decided, madly, to remake in their own image, dividing it into six precincts corresponding to Venice's six sectors, and with the same names. They built castles at Suda, Frangocastello and Spinalonga which faced, significantly, both ways – out to sea, to the enemy, and inland, to the enemy. They even built a version of their own Arsenal.

Needless to say, the Cretans were in a state of total rage and rebellion for the 460 years that the Venetians governed them. Venetian rule was so strict and so oppressive that that most literary of popes, Pius II, remarked 'As among brute beasts, aquatic creatures have the least intelligence, so among human beings the Venetians are the least just and the least capable of humanity.' Definitely not a good press for the Most Serene Republic.

It is amazing to think that the Venetians were able to hold Crete for so long. But they felt that they had no real choice. Crete fed them. For the one thing in which the Venetians were not self-sufficient was food. Since sugar was precious, the Venetians created on Cyprus what must have been the first sugar plantation, complete with black African slaves. Had this experiment worked out properly, Venice might today be known as 'the home of Dixieland Jazz'. The Venetians also went in for slave trading abroad. The men who rowed their galleys, interspersed with Venetians sentenced to hard labour by a

The Venetian fort of Belonia on Naxos. The silhouette of Mt. Zeus is visible in the distance.

Venetian influence
extended to the decoration
of tabernacles, such as this
example at Panormos,
Crete.

LEFT The approach to the
port of Khania, Crete,
which became part of the
Venetian Empire.

criminal court, were however 'Slavs', mostly from Dalmatia, who were paid wages on the return voyage. They also did well in running a clandestine canteen aboard the galleys taking pilgrims to the Holy Land. The ship's own kitchen was so bad that paying passengers would slip down below decks to buy food and even, one pilgrim reported, excellent wine, in which the German pilgrims over-indulged themselves. A not unsympathetic scene is repeated today in the taverns around St. Mark's.

Blackamoors began to appear in Venetian paintings as well as on furniture. There may be scholarly studies on the subject, but it would seem that black Africans in Venice were used as living ornaments for the rich, like some exotic pets today. Many of them became gondoliers, a possible explanation for the blackamoor in Bellini's *Miracle of the True Cross*. In 1622, a formidable Englishwoman, Althea, Countess of Arundel, who was living in the Mocenigo Palace (200 years before Byron) while her sons were studying at Padua's great university, heard that her name had been involved in a local political scandal. She, a foreign and unofficial guest, and a woman at that, demanded an audience with the Doge. She got it, as well as an apology, and a gift of sweetmeats and wax. When she returned to England, the Doge gave her permission to take back with her a gondola, together with a blackamoor. *Bravissima*, Althea.

There is an old Venetian saying: '*Coltivar el mare e lasser star la terra*'. This means 'cultivate the sea and let the land alone'. It was Doge Morosini who warned the Venetians about 'adventures' on the Italian mainland, conquering land and cities they did not need and could not garrison. But, in due course, the Venetians forgot their own good advice. They moved onto the mainland, and acquired the Alpine region of Friuli, where there was a good deal of timber for their ships – and an undistinguished family of apothecaries called Vidal. They also occupied the cities of Bergamo, Brescia and Verona.

In 1439, Venice hired Bartolomeo Colleoni, a mercenary warrior, to relieve the mainland city of Brescia, then under siege by the Duke of Milan. The general transported six galleys and twenty-five smaller supply boats up the Adige river and over Mount Altissimo to Lake Garda, surprising the Milanese troops and liberating the city. This miracle of transportation was achieved by using wooden platforms on wheels. The Milanese Duke was suitably impressed, and hired Colleoni to beat back the threatening French army of King Charles VII – sometimes known as Joan of Arc's mistake. Colleoni also accepted gold florins from a group of Florentine exiles who wanted to rid Florence of the Medici family; then, leaving the Medici strictly alone, he returned to Venice and became, in 1455, the Republic's highly paid commanding general, for life. When he was seventy-five, France's King Louis XI offered him 150,000 ducats a year – double his Venice stipend – but he

turned down this offer and remained in his castle near Bergamo, always on call to Venice.

When Colleoni was dying, Venice sent an official to see him. The great condottiere's last spoken words to Venice were, 'Beware of mercenaries. You don't know what harm I could have done you.' Colleoni bequeathed the Republic a large sum of money to erect, in front of St. Mark's, a bronze equestrian statue in his honour. The Republic's tax office promptly seized *all* of Colleoni's assets, which were reckoned to be at least equal to those of the Medici. But then, in a rare case of scruples, the State decided that it would spend one-tenth of the Colleoni ducats on the bronze statue. They brought from Florence the famous but aged sculptor, Andrea Verrocchio – Leonardo da Vinci's teacher – to design it. Verrocchio died before the bronze was cast, but what we see today is thought to be faithful to his design and to the image

The Miracle of the True Cross *by Gentile Bellini; an example of a 1494 news event being turned into a great painting. The Cross was being carried in procession across the Bridge of S. Lorenzo when the relic fell into the canal. Caterina Cornaro, ex-Queen of Cyprus, in crown and veil, is among the women watching the scene. The relic did not sink. Note the blackamoor on the right.*

of Colleoni, whose black eyes were described as being 'vivid, penetrating, and terrifying'. His last name, which he may have assumed when he began his military career, means 'testicles' in the Latin vulgate and exists as *coglioni* in modern Italian. Bartolomeo boasted of having three; this explains, perhaps, his inherent respect for the Medici family, whose coat-of-arms then bore three balls.

Until about one hundred years ago, no statue to a public figure could be set up anywhere in the city, let alone in St. Mark's Square. The State solved the problem of Colleoni's bequest by saying that 'in front of St. Mark's' could be legally interpreted to mean 'in front of the Scuola of St. Mark's', next to the Church of SS. Giovanni e Paolo. That is where the statue has stood since 1496, its subject and story illustrating two facets of Venetian history of the fifteenth century.

The famous equestrian statue of Bartolomeo Colleoni is considered to be the finest since antiquity. Designed by Andrea Verrocchio, this monument to Colleoni, the mercenary general who led Venice's army, stands in front of the Scuola of St. Mark's.

IV

THE MERCANTILE CITY
AND ITS PEOPLE

*From the first salt merchants, to the empire-builders, to the noble
families, wealth, not fame, was the spur. But then the Venetian
nobles, like their American counterparts, based their wealth and
glory proudly on trade. In this, both Venetians and Americans
part company with those European noble families who
disdained trade and based their nobility on land,
something not easy to do if you happen to live on water.*

THE Venetians never wanted an empire. They just wanted to do business –
and make money. Although there were fewer than 50,000 Venetians when
the eastern Roman Empire fell to the Crusaders, the Venetians managed to
end up with three-eighths of what remained of the old empire as well as
exclusive trading rights throughout the entire eastern Mediterranean. It was a
marvellous deal for the inhabitants of a few mudflats in an out-of-the-way
lagoon.

If Venice was the United States of its day, the Rialto was the Wall Street of
the Venetian world. Here deals were made, money was borrowed and lent,
ships and cargoes were sent round the world on a handshake. When Shylock,
in Shakespeare's *Merchant of Venice*, asks 'What news on the Rialto?', he could
have been referring to the current interest rate. Alas, the Bard of Avon, who
certainly knew Italy well (and cribbed the plot of his *Merchant of Venice* from a
story written by a Florentine, and not then translated into English), may be
partly responsible for some confusion in the English-speaking world ever
after. For the famous bridge is not itself 'the Rialto', but the bridge serving the
needs of the merchants and pedestrians of that 'high embankment' where the
city was first founded.

Venice's gold ducat was known and accepted as legal tender everywhere,
from London to Calcutta. Even the Venetians' nickname for the coin, *il
zecchino*, travelled abroad, where it was later to become corrupted into *sequin*.
(*Zecchino* is derived from *zecca*, the Italian word for the Mint which turned out
the bright, shiny coins.) Venice built its own Mint on the wharf opposite the

Doge's Palace, one of the first marble buildings in the city.

In its more prosperous years, the Venetian Republic did not have a State bank. Banks then were owned by patrician families. Since they frequently failed, due to mis-management, the Republic decided to abolish them in 1587; that same year, the government opened its own Banco della Piazza di Rialto, where today's fruit and vegetable market is held. It was a strangely un-Venetian operation, as neither bank nor client earned interest on funds; it was essentially a safety-deposit vault. In 1619, a merchant, who regularly supplied the Venice Mint with precious metals, demanded that he be paid half in gold and half in credit. Venice met his demand by opening the second State bank, called the Banco del Giro, *giro* meaning 'turning', or, more specifically, endorsing over to a third party. It was a banking innovation. A merchant's

Gabriele Bella's Il Bancho del Giro di Rialto. *Venice's second public bank was opened in 1619; for the first time in banking history, credit could be transferred from one account to another by means of an endorsement, or giro. Situated in the Rialto, near today's fruit and vegetable market, it afforded Bella a background for this tiny canvas, filled with milling Venetians.*

This bust of a noble lady of the Venetian aristocracy gazes wistfully from the windows of the State Archives.

credit in the bank could be transferred to another client on his spoken word – not all of the clients were literate – if done in the presence of witnesses.

When Gabriele Bella painted his view of the Banco del Giro more than one hundred years after it was founded, he may have been attracted to the subject because he could show a wide variety of contemporary Venetians doing what they liked best – milling about. Today this would be called 'calendar art', but, like Bella's other Venetian views, it is a valuable, as well as charming, document. No, he could not draw, but he was busy.

The Marcello family has been prominent in Venice for a thousand years. The head of the family today, and custodian of the family's archives, is Count Gerolamo Marcello. The archives fill several rooms and, as the Count says sadly, no one will ever be able to read them all. (Can a computer cope with a thousand volumes of handwritten documents, the hand being modified over the centuries?) In a ledger, dated 1529, the credits and debits of the Republic are recorded – Venetians were very serious about money. The name of one Nicolo Vidal appears – it is an old Venetian name – and this particular Vidal has achieved immortality through debt: he is recorded as owing 898 ducats. Many Vidals figure in Count Marcello's ledger book owing much money. Debits are a unifying thing in a family.

But what of the State Archives? In what used to be a monastery, there are thirty-six miles of shelving, a thousand years of history – turning to dust. The history of the Venetian Empire, of its great families, like the Tiepolos. In fact, the chief archivist today is a Tiepolo, and the last of her line. I asked if I could see the famous Book of Gold in which the names of the patrician families are recorded, the one book in which I lusted to see my own name illuminated. As she turned the ancient pages, I saw the great names in alphabetical order: Baglioni, Barbaro, Bembo, Bonini. . . . Would she never get past the 'B's?

The Book of Gold in the State Archives, wherein were inscribed the names of all the noble families in Venice until the Republic ended in 1797.

*The State Archives of the
Venetian Republic, housed
in a former monastery,
span a thousand years of
history — and thirty-six
miles of shelving.*

'*E la famiglia Vidal?*' I asked eagerly. '*Non era patrizio!*' she replied, with unwarranted relish. No Vidal was listed among the nobles.

Still, everyone who crosses Venice's Accademia Bridge, one of the three that span the Grand Canal, must walk through the Campo S. Vidal. Alongside it flows the Rio de S. Vidal, one of Venice's 176 small canals, whose principal task is to carry rubbish out to the Grand Canal for eventual distribution in the Adriatic Sea. Campo S. Vidal is a precinct run by dozens of Venetian cats (Shylock described their noble ancestors as being 'harmless and useful'). Supported by the locals, the cats are doing well. The Church of S. Vidal might also be said to be doing well. It has many visitors each day. But it is deconsecrated, like many other ancient but superfluous churches in Italy, and is now a commercial art gallery where concerts are also held.

Although the Venetians have a well-defined class system, they have never had a class war. There isn't enough space for one. There was barely enough space for the headquarters of the Venetian Empire. The hall in the Doge's Palace, where the Great Council met, was suitably magnificent, but the offices of the various departments of State were so many small cupboards containing yet more cupboards. As a result, the Venetians began to fill in their waterways. In the process, they spoiled the marvellous filtering system whereby, with each tide, the canals cleansed themselves and the city. The new streets were called Rio Terrà, 'canals filled in with earth', and the famous Riva degli Schiavoni is nearly twice as wide now as it was originally, when its bridges spread across the entire *riva*. Horizontal expansion was restricted by the number of tons of brick and marble that could be supported by the millions of wooden pilings, driven manually into the hard clay subsoil.

Also, Venice had a very important aspect of 'democracy' forced upon it unwittingly by the original settlers who chose to build a city in the middle of the sea. Apparently there have never been carriages in Venice, and the horse was banished centuries ago. The gondola was designed to transport a nobleman from the water-gate of his palace to that of another palace by the most direct water route. Originally, gondolas were richly decorated and came in many colours until, during a wave of austerity, it was decreed that all gondolas be painted black. (Detroit's Doge at the beginning of this century, Henry Ford, issued a similar decree: 'I don't care what colour the car is so long as it's black.') Unfortunately, over the years, the practice of filling in minor canals left a good many palaces land-locked. Ultimately, to reach St. Mark's Church, or the Doge's Palace, the noble was obliged to walk, and there is nothing more democratic than walking with the common folk, while keeping the uncommon touch. Although chroniclers do not mention the use of the sedan chair as a means of conveyance, something of that sort must have been used for the old and fragile. Today's Venice continues the democratic

The gondola was designed to transport the nobleman from the water-gate of his palace to that of another palace by the most direct water route.

The Palazzo Dario, built in the fifteenth century, is one of the smallest residences on the Grand Canal. Its Renaissance façade, the fanciful use of marble and inlaid discs, rosettes and plaques, may seem today to be almost whimsical, but rarely fails to delight the eye.

The Palazzo Dario, seen from the land entrance. This modest, compact house shows its earlier Gothic rear view in this picture. The Renaissance façade that faces the Grand Canal was later clamped on to this original structure.

tradition in this respect, for almost everyone crams himself into the crowded *vaporetti* – or walks. The handicapped are democratically treated as equals.

So there was some social mobility. Among the nobles it was decided by a reading of the family abacus who was to be in the upper reaches of the financial pyramid. Next came the 'citizen', who was likely to be a civil servant. Although a citizen's daughter could marry into a noble family, no noble daughter could marry beneath her rank. Should she not find a proper suitor, the gates of the nunnery yawned.

The noble Bianca Cappello fell in love with a poor Florentine clerk, posted in Venice, and ran off to Florence to live with him. A great beauty, she caught the eye of Grand Duke Francesco de' Medici, who built a house for her not far from his family's tasteful home, the Pitti Palace. The two houses were then connected by a tunnel to avoid unkind gossip and inclement weather. Eventually, the rats in the tunnel became such a nuisance that one dark night, Bianca's Florentine clerk was dispatched, with a knife, to his last posting. Freed of love, Bianca became Grand Duchess of Tuscany. The Venetians, sensing the possibility of improving trade with the rich Tuscan city, proudly styled her a 'true daughter of the Republic'. But before Bianca could sew-up any trade contracts, she and the Grand Duke died within hours of each other, probably from poison. And the fickle Venetians did not declare even one day of mourning for its 'true daughter'. Bianca holds the sixteenth-century female record for extremes of fortune on the Venetian social ladder.

A Venetian 'citizen', who held a job in the Doge's Palace similar to that of Under-Secretary for Trade, was sent on a mission to Constantinople. He returned with a favourable trade agreement, and enough bolts of cloth-of-gold, a gift from the Sultan, to put an awning over St. Mark's Square. Instead, he invested his new wealth, including a bonus from the Doge, in a relatively small Gothic house on the Grand Canal. He hired the architectural studio run by the Lombardi family to clamp a Renaissance marble facing over the exterior, and moved in. He was called Giovanni Dario; and his house, the Palazzo Dario, is a favourite 'sight' for tourists. Although he could have bought his way into the Book of Gold, he died not a nobleman but a 'citizen'.

Venice's working-class seems to have shared in the good times and the bad times of Venetian trade and power. If there was ever such a thing as a servant shortage, people from what is today called Yugoslavia were unnaturally eager to be domestic servants. Curiously, there were no dining rooms in Venetian palaces. Ballrooms could be converted into banqueting halls for great occasions. Otherwise, the family ate somewhere near the kitchen, joined at table by the servants who also waited on them. Even the houses with ballrooms were often otherwise cramped, with windows only on the front and the back.

Space – or its absence – to one side, class war would have been bad for the business of Venice Incorporated in which everyone plays a part, from the glassmaker to the bartender to what is left of the noble families, who still do what they have always done – survive through trade. In Venice, like it or not, everyone's in the same boat. And everyone is born knowing it. The engine room of that boat, where the civil servants kept things humming for many great centuries, can be visited in the Doge's Palace by special arrangement. The effect – in compactness – is not unlike the engine room of a modern submarine. The chances of a mutiny, or class war, on a smooth-running submarine are almost nil. No space, no *time*.

It was from the Doge's Palace, beside St. Mark's Church, that both the city and the Venetian empire were governed. But the Venetians thought of themselves as the heirs of the old Roman Republic, rather than of the later Roman Empire. They did not want an emperor – they had learned the lesson of Julius Caesar. Nor did they want a democracy – they had learned the lesson of Pericles. They wanted a state in which it was possible for those of good family to do well at business.

The Doge's Palace (Palazzo Ducale), the seat of government, seen from the island of S. Giorgio Maggiore.

FAR LEFT ABOVE
*The Great Council.
This is Gabriele Bella's
eighteenth-century view of
the assembly of all the
Venetian nobles in the
Doge's Palace. The Great
Council was not unlike
Britain's House of Lords.*

FAR LEFT BELOW
*Bella's painting of the
Council of Ten.
The smaller the
assembly, the greater was
the real power.*

LEFT *Bella's view of the
Three Inquisitors in their
chamber in the Doge's
Palace. This was where
most power was wielded.*

In the splendid hall of the Doge's Palace, the Great Council met. Every male Venetian of twenty-five or older, whose family was listed in the Book of Gold, was a member of the Great Council which governed Venice. Basically, it elected not only the Doge but all the other high officers of state. The Council also chose from its own members a number of committees, and these committees governed the Republic – and one another. First there was the Senate. Then there were the six councillors, one from each of the six sectors (*sestiere*) of the city, and finally there were three judicial magistrates. Together with the Doge, they formed the Council of Ten – the most powerful body in Venice. In 1539, when the enemies of the Republic were pressing in on all sides and quick decisions were needed, the Council of Ten was supplemented by a Council of Three – the Three Inquisitors.

The government of the day can be seen through the eyes of Gabriele Bella, perhaps the worst painter that Venice was ever to produce, who nevertheless left us with vignettes of life in Venice which no one else would have recorded. We see in his small canvases snapshot views of the entire assembly of the Great Council, and the Council of Ten, as awesome as ever, which, unless Bella got it wrong, consisted, very sensibly, of seventeen officials. Then we see Bella's Three Inquisitors, whose official task was to prevent the theft of State Secrets. In practice, they decided which of the accused should live and which should die. Or, as the Venetians used to whisper: 'The Ten send you to the torture chamber – the Three send you to your grave.'

The pointed Gothic arches of the east façade, which faces the central courtyard of the Doge's Palace. This was the first part of the palace to be rebuilt after a catastrophic fire in 1483. Here, costumed figures pose during Carnival-time in Venice.

The Book of Gold was shut for all time in 1297. Or so it was thought. The families inscribed in it had all achieved that noble status by being good traders and thereby becoming rich. No family was ever dropped from this Social Register, this Debrett's Peerage, spawned by import-export ledgers and shimmering with sequins. In the last two centuries of the Republic, many of the nobles were bankrupt. But they still attended the meetings of the Great Council, their robes of state hiding patched or ragged clothes, rather like today's hereditary British peers, taking the tube to the House of Lords.

In an odd way the founders of the American Republic were fascinated by the Venetian Republic, and there are some similarities between the two. Both accepted as perfectly natural human greed. Neither was filled with much spirit of mission or of ideology. That was why each republic made sure that it would never become a monarchy – or a democracy.

Venetian doge and American president have one thing in common: each swore to uphold a constitution in which were built many 'checks and balances' that would make it impossible, legally, for him to subvert the Republic. Whereas the American president has a Senate, a House of Representatives and a Supreme Court to counterbalance him, the doge had a Senate, a Council of Ten, and a Great Council. As a result, there was never, in the course of the millennium, a Venetian dictator. The United States still have eight centuries to go.

The term 'checks and balances' is relatively modern, but the Venetians most surely invented the system first. To outsiders, the Venetian government may have resembled a pyramid, with the doge perched on top, and the Great Council forming the base. But to elect the doge, the pyramid had to be inverted. When election day came, the 1,200 nobles in the Great Council gathered. The youngest was then told to go out into the square and bring back the first Venetian boy he found. The child's task was to draw names out of a hat or an urn – the same ritual used today for Italy's weekly lottery. One can imagine how many well-scrubbed children had been sent to the square by their mothers on that day. Mary McCarthy, in her *Venice Observed*, summed up the procedure: 'Out of the Great Council, nine were picked by lot to elect forty electors, who had to be chosen by a majority of at least seven. The forty drew lots to see which twelve would elect twenty-five more by a majority of at least seven. These twenty-five then drew lots to see which nine would elect forty-five by a majority of at least seven. Finally, these forty-five drew lots to choose eleven, who would vote for forty-one electors, who would elect the doge by a majority of at least twenty-five.' Thank you, Mary.

Sir Henry Wotton, the seventeenth-century British ambassador, claimed that the system had been invented by a Benedictine monk, but no election of the head of a religious order is as complicated and cautious as that. Even the election of the pope is more ordinary, with coffee-drinking cardinals chatting while seated on each other's conclave cots, or exchanging thoughts while shaving, and, finally, letting the Holy Ghost guide their hands when filling out the papal ballot. The Venetian system of choosing the West's only leader of Oriental splendour, one who even walked like a Chinese emperor under a golden umbrella, seems to have been invented by the kind of mind that created the Chinese puzzle of boxes-within-boxes.

At the time of the doge's coronation, he was given a list of all the things that he was *not* allowed to do. The most important thing that he was not allowed to do was govern Venice. The doge was the State incarnate; but he had no personal power. His letters, incoming and outgoing, were read by censors. No member of his family could hold public office. The only gifts he could accept from foreign potentates were items like rose-water and balms. His wife was

The Tetrarchs. These four figures are set on a corner of the Treasury tower of St. Mark's Church, and are thought to be Syrian work of the fourth century. Venetians call them 'The Moors', probably because of the dark red colour of the carved porphyry.

This painting by Gabriele Bella shows the presentation of the newly-elected doge to the people, assembled in St. Mark's Church.

Today, the fruit and vegetable market is held on the
site of the first Banco della Piazza di Rialto. Here
housewives and restaurant owners come to pick and
choose from that day's delivery from the mainland.
The clock on the Church of S. Giacomo can be seen in
the background.

expected to be without blemish, although she had no official role to play. When the doge left the palace on State occasions, he was accompanied by two councillors, who made sure that he did not overstep his bounds by word or deed. He was the only citizen of the Venetian Republic ever to have a noble title – Most Serene Prince – his fellow nobles being addressed simply as 'nobleman'. The large number of today's Venetian counts and countesses were created either during the Austrian occupation, which was immediately followed by the brand new Kingdom of Italy (1866), or, more sensibly, by themselves.

Doge comes from the Latin *dux*, which gives us 'duke' and which gave the Italians, from 1922 to 1945, *Il Duce* – Benito Mussolini, the fascist dictator. Although elected for life, nineteen of the first fifty doges were executed, blinded or banished. The excuse for oustings was rarely corruption; usually, the unfortunate prince had either lost a battle or, worse, an important trade contract. After 1423, the doges were encouraged to die of natural causes.

Although a Republic can be almost anything in practice, the Venetian Republic was – and is – remarkably consistent in its sense of self. Like the Jews, the Venetians were a minority in a generally hostile world. In 1508, Pope Julian II extorted a pledge from the French King Louis XII to involve France in a costly war against tiny Venice. (Julian was the pope who commissioned Michelangelo to paint the Sistine Chapel.) Instigated by Julian II, who wanted to guarantee his hold on the Adriatic port of Ancona, the Holy League of Cambrai was formed to crush the Venetian Republic. The official reason for the hatred of Venice was that it was 'treasonously' doing business with Moslem countries, on the famous principle 'Venetians first, Christians second'. Not only were the Venetians doing business with various Sultans – including an offer in 1508 to dig the Suez Canal – but their trade pacts with them were virtual monopolies. The result of the war waged by the League of Cambrai against Venice was that the Pope regained control of the Romagna region (perhaps best known to summer tourists for Rimini and to others for Federico Fellini), and various other mainland cities, most of which later returned voluntarily to Venetian rule.

V

THE TURNING
OF THE TIDE

*Even the most neatly balanced political system can become
unbalanced by external enemies. When Christian Constantinople
fell to the Moslem Turks in 1453, the tide began to turn. Venice
and the whole of Europe was threatened by this Evil Empire.*

THROUGHOUT the last 600 years of its existence, the Venetian Empire
feared, most of all, the Turks and the Spanish, not for religious or
ideological reasons, but for business reasons. Today it is the Emperor of the
West, President Ronald W. Reagan, who tells his people that the Soviet
Union is the 'Evil Empire' (they do not put 'In God We Trust' on their
kopeks), and the Pentagon-CIA tells everyone who will listen that America's
greatest immediate danger comes from the Spanish-speaking two-thirds of
the two American continents.

Venetians relied on their fleet, on their wealth, on their cunning.
Particularly cunning was their placement of strategic defence systems.
Complex forts, like those in Greece, were built to protect the Venetian seas –
and the 'Free World'. For the next two centuries there was war – at sea and on
land – from one end of the Mediterranean to the other, while back home, the
Republic's PR boys went into high gear. Even the churches celebrated the far-
flung empire with replicas of military bases, such as those on the façade of S.
Maria del Giglio. The church was ready to rejoice at God's love for Venice,
for now they were 'Christians first, and Venetians second'. The Pope also
rejoiced when Venice won a victory over the Turks at sea. And yet, along
with most other European monarchs, he no doubt secretly celebrated when
Venice lost a battle or lost control of a dominion. Venetians always needed to
be taken down a notch or two.

But it was the Republic, not God, that was obliged to fight the war. The
Doge's Palace was White House, Pentagon, State Department and CIA all
rolled into a single, beautiful, unfortified building. There is one immutable
law of government: the more money you spend on intelligence and counter-
intelligence, the less you know about what's going on in the world. The CIA in
America, at Langley, Virginia, spends billions of dollars and yet the American

*S. Maria del Giglio. This Venetian church, near the
Gritti Palace, is one of the few in Christendom to
depict military installations. This bas-relief map on the
front façade is of a Venetian fortress at Corfu. Statues
of the Barbaro family fill the niches in the walls, for
they paid for this sumptuous work to be carried out
in exaltation of the naval and political glories of
their family.*

*The Secret Chancellery
in the Doge's Palace.*

Government seldom has a clue as to what is going on in the world. The Venetians were more frugal – and more clever – than the Americans.

In one little room of the Doge's Palace, three Venetian gentlemen, the Three Inquisitors, operated as the directors of intelligence and counter-intelligence. The Most Serene Republic was well served by them, and they knew indeed what their enemies were up to. But then intelligence is the key to just about everything. The more anyone knows the better off he is. The more a State knows – particularly a small, beleaguered State – the better off *it* is. From all over the world, Venetian ambassadors sent home information, while Venetian spies ferreted out other countries' secrets. And Venetian agents took care of Venetian enemies.

In the sixteenth century, the Three Inquisitors engaged one Agostino Amadi to make them a code book. Thousands of his codes were used to send messages back and forth from every corner of Europe and Asia. Constructed from ingenious sheets, or sometimes interlocking wheels of paper, pierced with holes, these codes, when placed over an innocuous letter and aligned with a particular word would reveal the secret message to be gleaned from those words pinpointed by the holes. All these codes gave the Venetians intelligence and knowledge, which they converted into power.

At the time when Amadi was concocting these codes, Leonardo Loredan was the Doge of a Venice the world still envied. This serene nobleman ruled the city at a time when Venice had no cause to be most serene. Loredan's immediate predecessor, Doge Agostino Barbarigo, had presided over the opening of the beautiful Renaissance church of S. Maria dei Miracoli, the installation of the clock in St. Mark's Square, and he attended the world première, or unveiling, of Carpaccio's cycle of pictures of the *Legend of St. Ursula*. Yet his reign ended not only in scandal and corruption, but with the news that Vasco da Gama, after discovering the route to India around the Cape of Good Hope, had returned to Portugal with ships laden with spices. The news was a death knell in the Rialto. Venice's near-monopoly on the spice trade had ended.

Doge Barbarigo also closed Venice's 150-year-old red-light district at Castelletto, near the Rialto, as well as the Bridge of Teats, where prostitutes plied their trade. Some of the women had become educated, even learned; and preferred to be called not whores, but courtesans. Some were deeply patriotic. When a seventy-year-old Secretary of the Senate confided State Secrets to one of the courtesans, she denounced him to the Ten. In due course, his body was seen hanging in front of the Doge's Palace.

After Doge Barbarigo's death, the Inquisition opened an inquiry into the Doge's affairs. They found that he had been extorting funds, smuggling cargoes into Venice, and cheating the Treasury. Leonardo Loredan was

elected for his personal probity. Ironically, it was with Doge Loredan that Venice moved into the beginning of her decadence.

Marino Sanudo records that at this time there were 11,654 registered (and taxed) courtesans in the city. Although the wealthy ones were not without power, they were apparently unable to persuade the authorities to control their principal competition: transvestites from the mainland. Thoroughly miffed, the Venetian courtesans began dressing like the transvestites but, as silicone injections had not been invented, they also could proudly expose their breasts while seated in their windows. One of the Doge's relatives was killed by another patrician in a fight over a courtesan's favours. Moral fibre was plainly weakening in the early 1500s: a Venetian archbishop was arrested for counterfeiting ducats, and the Senate debated allowing, upon payment of only 2,000 ducats, certain men to wear the senatorial toga in public – but without the right to vote. Doge Loredan privately told rich nobles that if they would make a cash donation to the depleted treasury, their generosity would be made public after his death – and they might thus be rewarded with the doge's cap.

Under Doge Loredan, two young artists, Giorgione and Titian, were commissioned to paint the façade of the Fondaco dei Tedeschi, the Venetian emporium used by Teutonic merchants in the Rialto as their hostel and warehouse. Loredan also engaged Giorgione to paint *indoor* frescoes on the ground floor of his new palace, which the family had to sell in 1581. It is known today as the Vendramin Palace; here Richard Wagner died, and here the winter gambling casino is housed. Doge Loredan died a slow and painful death of gangrene at the age of eighty-five. The Republic also was dying, but of a malady more leisurely and sorrowful than painful.

In the State Archives there is a book marked '*Secreta – Secretissima*'. That means 'Top Secret', 'Eyes Only', 'Burn on Sight'. It contains the secret orders of State, and responses to requests. There is one from Brother Johannes di Ragusio. He proposed to the Council that for 1,500 ducats a year for life, he would kill anybody they wanted him to, and not be caught. He had developed, according to his petition, new ways of poisoning people and he put himself at the disposal of the Council. A vote was taken. Ten of them, the book records, said 'Yes' to Brother John. Six were cautious and said 'No'. So they agreed to take him on at 1,500 golden ducats a year but, being good Venetians, there was to be a trial period. So they suggested in a little footnote – why doesn't he have a go at killing the Holy Roman Emperor?

The torture chambers were in the Doge's Palace, conveniently near the Inquisitors' chamber. Here enemies of the State were strangled, beheaded, drowned. Always in secret. The neatness and proximity of these facilities is another indication of how ship-shaped the Venetian government was.

Everything that mattered, and was not for show, took place in a series of small compartments, often adjacent one to the other. Here, justice was meted out, sometimes with undue haste (so unlike today's Italy). The accused, most likely a fellow-Venetian, was sentenced, and then, a few yards away, either tortured or executed within minutes. It was all very economical and brisk. And the Ship of State, kept to its true, profitable course, sailed serenely on.

You never really knew who had been executed until you happened to see his body hanging upside down in front of the palace. It might be your husband or your father. William Lithgow, a sixteenth-century traveller who claimed to have tramped 36,000 miles, tells in his account of his adventures (*The Totall Discourse of the Rare Adventures and painful Peregrinations of long Nineteene Years*) of landing in Venice in 1609 at the Molo, next to the Doge's Palace, and seeing 'a great throng of people, and in the midst of them a great smoake'. The Republic was roasting a Franciscan friar 'for begetting fifteen young Noble Nunnes with child, and all in one year – he being also their father-confessor'. These 'Noble Nunnes' were probably in the convent attached to the Church of S. Zaccaria, which was first built in the ninth century. By the time the friar had become a father, it was an entirely new church with a splendid sixteenth-century Renaissance façade. It was also probably the richest church in town, owning all of what today is St. Mark's Square. Its benefices included the presence of scores of young noble girls whose parents, perhaps, could not find a dowry or a husband for their daughters. They became reluctant 'brides of Christ'. But something inexplicable took place. They were allowed to entertain young swains of their own rank within the convent's walls. They even held mixed balls. The convent's fame spread like honey across the upper crust of Europe and many a young man set out on a devout pilgrimage to S. Zaccaria, said to hold the remains of John the Baptist's father. If William Lithgow's information was correct – and foreigners landing in Venice for the first time tend to be confused by many things – more should be known about the Franciscan brother who became a father fifteen times in one year. It is just possible that he, having easy access to the convent, was blamed for the busy-ness of the noble lay visitors. After all, the Noble Nunnes did not want to betray their own class, and thus lose their terrestrial bridegrooms. When things finally got too riotous in the convent, it was shut down.

The two columns in the Piazzetta between the Doge's Palace and the Sansovino Library (originally the Republic's Mint), were brought to Venice from the Middle East in the twelfth century. Both are carved from a single piece of granite, and the red column has been identified as being of Anatolian granite. The Venetians actually brought three columns home, but one rolled off the ship and has never been found, which probably seemed just as well at

The Church of S. Zaccaria. This fifteenth-century structure was built over a ninth-century church (part of which can be seen in the always-flooded crypt), and is considered to be a leading example of Venetian Renaissance design. When it was begun in 1444, the Gothic influence was still visible in the lower part of the façade. Forty years later, when Mauro Coducci, a second architect, had completed the façade, Venetian Renaissance was already a style of its own.

The torture chamber in the Doge's Palace. The noose, though used for proper and urgent hangings, was more commonly used to hang a suspected culprit by his feet, to encourage the desired confession of guilt.

the time, since no one could figure out what to do with the two remaining ones. Eventually, the Doge offered a 'suitable' reward to anyone who could raise the two columns. A local builder, Nicola Staratonio, who had built the Rialto's first wooden bridge, accepted the challenge and, in 1172, put the columns on their pedestals, where they still stand today. When asked what he wanted as his reward, he told the Doge he sought Venice's first gambling concession, gambling then being forbidden. His request was granted, and he was told that he could run a gaming-place between his two columns. Not a bad location, it must have seemed to Nicola, since it offered him and his hired hands the chance to fleece pilgrims and drunken sailors minutes after they had landed on the Molo. Venice's first gambling casino was probably a stall, or perhaps only a table, and the name of the game might have been to guess under which shell the bean was hidden.

However, the Doge also decided that the area between the two columns would be the suitable place for public executions and the columns themselves suitable places to hang, upside down, the bodies of men who had been executed within his palace. As the columns became a showplace for the remains of those who had incurred the Republic's wrath, Nicola's gambling venture fared badly: clients complained of being bled on, and games of chance lost their allure in so stern a setting.

Some years later a statue, said to represent St. Theodore (in dialect *Todaro*), was placed on one column, and St. Mark's lion was placed on the other. What is called a winged lion is actually a bronze chimera, probably from the fourth century BC, which could have been Chinese, Persian, or Assyrian in origin. (Another bronze chimera was found about 400 years ago in Tuscany and probably belonged to the Etruscans, a pre-Roman people who may have reached Italy from Assyria, as has been suggested by their language.) The St. Theodore statue is a collage of more than one Roman statue, assembled in the fourteenth century. The handsome head has been attributed to the era of the Emperor Hadrian, and a dragon sits beneath the figure's feet. Theodore had been the Venetians' first patron saint, their protector, until his place was usurped by the bones of St. Mark. The Evangelist may have wound up with a splendid tomb, beyond even his mother's wildest dreams, but Theodore still holds an enviable, commanding position. He is a marble composite like the urban composition he surveys.

Although torture and summary execution were standard procedures, they were not all that common. The rulers of Venice were the first to realise that the most effective means of controlling a people are psychological, through subtle intimidation.

The Council of Ten had many powers and responsibilities and one of them was to keep a watchful eye on the aristocracy of the city. Sometimes, quite arbitrarily, one of them would be summoned. 'Present yourself to the Council of Ten next Friday.' The nobleman would have a good week to worry. Then he would report to the ante-chamber, where he might sit on one of the uncomfortable wooden benches which line the walls, or he might pace up and down, nervously wondering what on earth it was that he had done. So the nobleman would have his day in the waiting-room, and then an official would come out and say, 'They don't want to see you – you can go home now.' They had made him sweat, which was plainly the object of the enterprise. When you don't have a large police force, you must find psychological ways of intimidating your citizens.

Like Florence, Venice had a letter-box where anonymous denunciations could be placed. Should the accusation prove to be untrue, the accuser would be found out – and punished. It was in Florence that the most famous case of a poison-pen letter to the authorities took place. Young Leonardo, newly-arrived in the big city from Vinci, was accused, along with others, of engaging in abhorrent sexual practices with local boys. He and his friends were summoned, questioned, preached to, and sent away. The anonymous accuser could well have been a professional rival who wanted Leonardo banished from Florence. This sort of accusation was less common in Venice because the Inquisitors prided themselves on the thoroughness of their investigations. If they were convinced that the charge was a false one, they would find the accuser – so much for anonymity – and charge *him*. The charges that most excited the Inquisition concerned security – State Secrets.

When the Inquisition in Rome accused the Venetians of not burning enough Jews as heretics, the Venetians serenely replied that as the Jews had never been Christian to begin with, they could hardly be heretics. The Venetians were nothing if not practical. Their principal trade was with the East where the Jews had many connections, so the Venetians used the Jews as they did everyone. On the other hand, the Republic kept a cold and watchful eye on the *marranos* – those Jews who had converted to Christianity. It was always feared that they might be crypto-infidels. Venetians may have been without scruples in trade and war, but they would not tolerate dissemblers in or outside their Ghetto.

When the powerful Catholic monarchs, Isabella and Ferdinand, expelled the Jews from Spain in 1492 (and from Portugal five years later), one of the reasons was to get rid of the *marranos*, many of whom had risen to high positions in the church hierarchy. These converts were always suspected of remaining Jews at heart, and of frequenting non-converted Jews and even synagogues. The Spanish Inquisition, and the two Iberian rulers, found their Holy Solution in expelling *all* Jews from their lands, including the *marranos* – which means 'swine'. The Jews and the *marranos* knew that the international

The Ghetto. The main square in the Jewish ghetto has a handsome well-head, an old people's home for the Jewish community, the Jewish museum and the oldest of the three existing synagogues. Because the Jews were required to live only in the ghetto district (so-named because foundries once stood there – gettare means to cast metal) from 1527, they had to add extra storeys to their buildings, making them the highest blocks of flats in Europe.

port-cities of Amsterdam and Venice were reputed to be places of tolerance and of welcome to outsiders. Venice was particularly attractive for two reasons. After the Spanish Inquisition, the Jews decided that they could not do business with Christian nations. The word of the Christian was not to be trusted, and promises at the baptismal font were not kept. The Jews' semitic brothers, the Moslems of the Ottoman Empire, told them that they would be well-received there. So, for some, Venice was to be a re-fuelling stop on their way to the Middle East – and to freedom. The other reason why so many opted for Venice, or the Venice-route eastwards, was that they had heard tales of Venice not unlike the tales travellers still tell. It was a beautiful city, well-governed by contemporary standards. Though Venice had a strict rule-book and many rules, some of them could be negotiated if one proved to be a useful citizen. It was a paradise where the gates were always ajar for the bright entrepreneur, the able middle-man.

Jews had been living in Venice at least from the 1300s, judging by the fact that in 1396 the Doge rented them some desolate land on the Lido as a cemetery, a decision probably backed up by the local Health Department since they could not be buried in Christian cemeteries, and the corpses somehow had to be disposed of. The early Jews gravitated towards the Rialto and became pawnbrokers and bankers, charging lower interest rates than the Christian money-changers. Legally, they could only be money-lenders or dealers in used cloth (as, later, in the Rome ghetto).

In 1516, all Venetian Jews were obliged to move to the Ghetto Nuovo (or 'new foundry') district, next to the Ghetto Vecchio. When the population grew, they were allowed to add more floors to the rented buildings, up to seven stories – possibly the highest in Europe by the year 1541. And in 1633, they were allowed to occupy another block of buildings known as the Ghetto Nuovissimo – the site of the last Venetian foundry before all such activity was concentrated within the fortress-like walls of the Arsenal.

The Jewish community not only had to observe a curfew, but they had to pay the wages of the Christian keepers of the Ghetto gates which, apart from confining the Jews, also offered them protection from the rare anti-Jewish flare-ups among the Venetian rabble – perhaps sparked by that familiar tale that they ate Christian *bambini* with relish. Outside the Ghetto, they had to wear red hats. Curiously enough, they were allowed to practise medicine, and the Doge's official physician was often a Jew. Jewish doctors eventually obtained the right to visit even lesser patients without wearing the red hat.

Even though the Venetians were exporting the newly-invented rosaries throughout the Islamic countries (a ship's bill of lading in 1561 includes '10 crates of rosaries' for Alexandria), their vaunted sense of toleration did not include proselytising by Venetian Jews. When a report, perhaps unfounded,

*The five domes of
St. Mark's Church.
Originally much lower, in
Byzantine style, they were
topped in the fourteenth
century with their lead
outer domes, creating this
picturesque silhouette.*

that resident blackamoors were being circumcised in the Ghetto, reached the Doge's Palace, someone wrote, 'you who were born black and could have become a Christian, why did you choose to become a Jew?'

Meanwhile, back at the Ottoman Empire, despite profitable trading, Venice was on the defensive. Thanks to Sultan Mehmet (Mohammed) II, known as The Conqueror, Venice was to be on the defensive for most of the Republic's remaining history. Mehmet became Sultan of the Ottoman Empire in 1451; two years later, he captured Constantinople, and the Roman Empire of the East – the fabulous Byzantium – was at an end. But the infidel Sultan behaved better towards the people and the city than previous conquerors. Certainly, he behaved better than the Christian Crusaders who, led by Venetians, had plundered the city in 1203, taking much of the loot that Constantine – the man who had made the world safe for Christianity a thousand years earlier – had chosen to bring from Rome. The famous bronze horses, which today can be seen prancing over the main door of St. Mark's Church, are thought to have begun their prancing in Greece; they then moved on to Rome where they decorated the Emperor Trajan's Triumphal Arch before Constantine took them to his brand new city and set them up in the hippodrome, from whence the Venetians brought them home, along with anything else that caught their fancy.

Rethimnon, Crete, passed into Ottoman hands in 1669. This wall plaque remains as evidence of Turkish domination over the Greek islands.

*Bellini's portrait of Sultan Mehmet II. The powerful
Eastern ruler asked the Doge to send him Bellini to be
his court painter for a few years, and this portrait is
one of the few extant results of the artist's Turkish
sojourn. Mehmet was pleased with the portrait and
rewarded the painter handsomely, as did the Venetians
when Bellini returned home from his artistic good-will
mission.*

Mehmet II destroyed little of Constantinople. The major church of St. Sophia (where the Doge Enrico Dandolo, leader of the devastating Fourth Crusade, was buried) was simply converted to a mosque, and, on the site of the Church of the Holy Apostles, the model for Venice's St. Mark's, he built another mosque. Christians were allowed to worship in the remaining churches. Mehmet II showed much more tolerance than the pagan Roman and Christian Venetian conquerors. He was a cosmopolite, spoke six languages, and his sense of humour is recorded – which cannot be said of many of the 120 doges of Venice. In the 1470s, he asked Venice to 'lend' him Gentile Bellini to paint some pictures in Istanbul. Bellini was dispatched, together with two assistants, as the Venetians were interested in buttering-up the Sultan at that time. Besides, there was another Bellini waiting in the wings, Giovanni, who completed the 'history of Venice' that his brother was then painting in the Great Hall of the Doge's Palace. Gentile spent about a year in Turkey. The Sultan gave him a knighthood, some finery, a gold chain, and a life pension. The portrait of the Sultan (National Gallery, London) and a watercolour of a Turkish scribe (Gardner Collection, Boston) are just about all that is left of Bellini's mission abroad.

During the next century, between 1540 and 1571, the Turks were to conquer Nauplia, Naxos, the Cyclades, and the great island of Cyprus. After Venice's troubles with her European enemies had been sorted out, her trade with the East reached a peak in the years 1559–64. Cyprus was the key to the renewed prosperity. The young Leonardo Donà, who was to become doge in 1606, came across an old letter, written in 1501 by Lt. Cosimo Pasqualigo, from Cyprus, to Leonardo Loredan.

This kingdom of Cyprus is of such importance to your state that if it fell into the hands of the enemy, which we have reason to fear, we may say that we have lost the ability to navigate in the Levant, and that we shall lose the shipping and trade there which are the very sinews and foundations of your Lordship's state. You fully understand that the advantages of this island, from which salt, cotton, and other merchandise are drawn every year, are the reason why our ships continue with the voyage to the Levant, especially because it is near to Syria, and convenient for all who go to that region, or to Alexandria. Hence we may conclude that this place is the most vital of your possessions and the most important to the preservation of your state. Therefore, we must seek to conserve it as a thing most precious to us.

After losing Cyprus to the Turks, Venice appealed to Pope Pius V to use his influence to rally the stronger Christian nations against the Ottoman forces and, while they were at it, against the spread of Islam. Spain's King Philip II deliberately dallied for two years, perhaps wanting to prolong the pleasure given him by Venice's loss; but, finally, the Battle of Lepanto was fought and

This contemporary rendition of the Battle of Lepanto gives an exciting visual account of the confrontation between the Turks and the protectors of Christendom.

won by the Venetian and Spanish fleets, with a little help from the Papal States and Genoa. The combined Christian fleet comprised more than 300 ships, of which 208 were galleys, which were more manoeuvrable as instruments of war. The Turks had the same number of ships, of which more than 250 were galleys, manned by 15,000 Christian slaves. In the battle 8,000 Christians died and 20,000 Moslems. The West was safe – for the time being. The naval victory in the Gulf of Lepanto is still considered today to have been a crucial one for keeping the Ottoman Empire from conquering Italy, its avowed goal, and for preserving Christianity in Europe. The victory seems all the more remarkable since the Christians' supreme naval commander was Don John, of landlocked Austria; he was born in equally landlocked Bavaria, son of Fraulein Barbara Blomberg, fathered by Spain's Charles V, and given recognition, and his Austrian title, by Philip II. He served his adopted country as captain of anti-pirate sea patrols in the Mediterranean, but Lepanto was the only mark he left upon history. It is curious that the places where great decisive battles are fought and won by the heroes somehow then 'disappear' as geographical entities, remaining only in history books. How many people now know where to find on their maps Trafalgar and Waterloo, let alone Lepanto?

Several churches were built in Italy to commemorate the winning of the Battle of Lepanto, and the Pope was given a Turkish flag seized by the victors as a souvenir. There was a rather shrill outcry in the 1970s by Roman Catholic traditionalists, when the late Pope Paul VI, in a gesture of good-will and ecumenism, decided to return the battle-scarred Turkish flag to the Patriarch of Istanbul. But Paul was a Lombard, not a Venetian. Lepanto was the last major battle where all ships were oar-propelled, and like so many 'great battles' in history, the footnote tells us more. Venice indeed again held Cyprus, but two years later, they returned the island to the Turks; so much for the 28,000 men who had lost their lives in the chess-game war between Christians and Moslems.

In the next century, the Turks laid siege to Heraklion in Crete. Christian Crete was part of the booty when the European Christians captured Constantinople. In dividing the spoils, the island, which ranks in size after Corsica in the Mediterranean, was given to Boniface, the Marquis of Montferrat. He promptly sold it to the Venetians, which may have been the covert clause in the contract from the start. And the 250,000 Cretans remained Venetian for more than 400 years. Most of those years were prosperous for both Venice and her dominions, but the Cretans wanted to switch empires. First, they hoped that the Maritime Republic of Genoa would conquer them and relieve them of Venetian 'oppression', but that task eventually fell to the Turks, who seemed to be in no hurry to acquire the island. In 1645, the Turks

FRAN:co MOROS: NI CAP:N GNALE INSEGVISCE L'ARMATA TVRCA, CHE FVGGE SEBENE PIV' NVMEROSA ASSAI DELLA VENETA, ARRIVA DVE DELLE PIV' GROSSE GALERE, E LE PRENDE.   APRILE 1689.

finally invaded; but it was not until twenty years later that they seized the capital city, Candia; and it was not until 1715 that the last Cretan islet still held by Venice fell to the Turks. The reluctant conquerors turned out to be the worst governors the Cretans had ever had. (The best, according to the Cretans, were the Egyptians, led by an Albanian pasha, in the nineteenth century.) On the surface, Crete seems to have had an unlucky history, but it is good to remember the words which the constitutionally uncharitable St. Paul (who had travelled there) said to St. Titus, quoting an even older judgement: 'The Cretans are always liars, evil beasts, and slow bellies.'

For twenty-two years the Venetian garrison had withstood the enemy, Crete being Venice's last bastion. When Crete fell in 1669, the Venetian Empire was effectively ended. What had been acquired and held through cunning and resourcefulness was lost, in the end, to brute force and Islam.

Francesco Morosini and the Venetian fleet encounter Turkish opposition during the naval battle at Morea, April 1689.

VI

THE FLOWERING
OF THE ARTS

*A city is like any other living organism. It is born, it grows,
it reproduces itself and it dies. Or adjusts to new conditions.
Venice was once a world capital. Now it is a sort of Disneyland,
but the city itself has changed little. Only the people who lived
here then are not here now. They are gone. And, obviously,
with time, all things age.*

EVEN SO, here on these islands in the lagoon, the twentieth century is kept
firmly at bay. What we see today is pretty much what people have seen
for centuries. Take the Ca' d'Oro, or House of Gold. It was built in the
fifteenth century, in Venice's golden age, which has long since vanished along
with its Serene Republic, its vast maritime empire, its glory and legendary
wealth. The shell of Venice is as it used to be, but inside the shell, all is changed.
Inside the Ca' d'Oro today there is an austere museum with whitewashed
walls, the building having been restored by a local nobleman, the Baron
Franchetti, who then donated it, together with his art collection, to the Italian
Republic. Only armed nightwatchmen live now in the House of Gold. The
inner spirit has fled along with its creators.

Most of the other palaces along the Grand Canal are equally deceptive. The
Palazzo Dario, for instance, is as showy in its own way as the Ca' d'Oro. But
again, it is all exterior. In fact, during the late nineteenth century it was a
boarding house, much frequented by American bachelors, while in the
twentieth century it was, for a time, the property of the manager of 'The
Who'. It is now said to be a kind of condominium, where subscribing
members, usually rich foreigners, can reserve for themselves an apartment, or
an entire floor, for a few weeks each year.

Practically all the Venetian palaces we see today were built 500 years ago,
when time stopped, at a moment of splendour, like a cinematic freeze-frame.

During the first ten days in June, from the sixteenth to the nineteenth
century, most able-bodied idle men in Venice found they had a lot of heavy
work to do. By 13 June, the Feastday of St. Anthony of Padua, every Venetian

The Coronation of the Virgin
*by Andrea di Bartolo,
from the Franchetti Collection
in the Ca' d'Oro
(ca' is an abbreviation of
casa meaning 'house').*

family with a villa on the mainland had left their palaces on the Grand Canal – usually as empty as possible. Everything that wasn't nailed down, or part of the palace's structure, was packed onto a barge, which then floated off to the country villa – and was then barged back again in the autumn. The building of mainland villas was a radical departure from Venetian convention and what had, for centuries, also been Venetian folk wisdom. Venice had been described in medieval times as a Land of Oz where man '*non arat, non seminat, non vidimiat*'. To which non-believers then probably asked, 'How do they survive?'

Mainland property was either bought or simply seized from a local lord or bishop, and many a gracious summer house was built, far from the summer stench and mosquitoes of Venice. Here the hired man could finally 'plow, sow, and make wine'. The introduction from America of Indian maize or corn (which was named *gran turco*, because of its resemblance to the great turbans of the Turkish enemy) changed Venetian attitudes towards farming on the mainland. Country estates could provide food and drink for a family and its retainers throughout the year, while the surplus could be sold during the winter from the water-gate entrances to the palaces on the Grand Canal.

It was fortunate for Venice, and later for the world, that the architect Andrea Palladio was born in the eighth year of the sixteenth century in Padua. During that century, he was kept busy building country houses for Venetian nobles who were now, very seriously, becoming landed gentry. His villas dot the Veneto mainland and even those not designed by him are usually, and correctly, called 'Palladian'.

For me, the most haunting of all these villas is at Maser, where Palladio built a villa for the two Barbaro brothers – the Most Reverend Daniele, patriarch-bishop of Aquilea, and Marcantonio, a diplomat. A Venetian palace in the city, no matter how splendid, was always a place of work. It was the family's headquarters for trade or even a warehouse. But now the Venetians were on the mainland, and everything was changed.

Officially, Villa Barbaro at Maser is a farmhouse, but plainly it is a house for pleasure. The heirs were spending the money that their hustler forebears had made. The architecture, the sculpture, reflect the change in Venetian mood. It is light, airy, classical, harmonious, and balanced. Nothing Byzantine here. This is Imperial Rome reborn. Here, a great architect, Palladio, and a great painter, Veronese, joined forces to create . . . well, for once all the adjectives of the guidebooks are inadequate.

The construction of the villa began around 1560 and the result was a happy collaboration between the two artists, whom the Barbaro brothers numbered among their friends. It must be said, however, that Veronese's contribution to Villa Barbaro has given the place its fame.

The early fifteenth-century façade of the Ca' d'Oro. The approach by gondola.

ABOVE The pavilion in the grounds of the Villa Barbaro at Maser.

RIGHT The Neptune grotto at the Villa Barbaro, which boasts a ceiling painted by Veronese.

RIGHT The Villa Barbaro at Maser, a Venetian family's simple summer retreat on the mainland. The classical exterior bears the unmistakable imprint of its architect, Andrea Palladio, while Paolo Veronese created the trompe l'oeil *frescoes inside.*

The real magic of the
Villa Barbaro is within.
Here, Veronese himself is
seen stepping somewhat
hesitantly through a
painted doorway. He has
arrived home after a day's
hunting. Is he late?

The harmony between the two artists working at Maser is well-chronicled, including a report by Giorgio Vasari who saw the Veronese frescoes while they were still 'fresh'. Yet in Palladio's own accounts of his architecture, he never mentions Veronese. Of Maser, Palladio wrote: 'That part of the building that stands rather forward, has two suites of rooms. The floor of the rooms above is on the same level with the pavement of the courtyard at the back where, cut into a hill, opposite the house, is a fountain with innumerable stucco-decorations and paintings. The fountain forms a small pond for fish and from there fresh water reaches the kitchen and serves to irrigate the gardens. The façade of the main house has four Ionic columns'. He also neglected to mention that Maser is his only villa of that period without a portico; nor does he mention that the Neptune grotto in the garden has a ceiling painted by Veronese.

The real magic at Maser is inside. In these rooms nothing is what it seems. Is that a real column or is it painted? Is that a real window? And even stranger are the Veronese people. There, almost life-size in a doorway, is a real, somewhat irritable woman – said to be a likeness of the painter's mistress. She looks towards the far end of a series of rooms, where a man, Veronese, is seen stepping through another door. He has been out hunting. Is he late? From a *trompe l'oeil* balcony an old woman, possibly the Barbaro nanny, is addressing the lady in blue, thought to be Marcantonio's wife. Veronese also included the family's favourite dog and pet parrot. Although dead for four centuries, they are all still alive in these rooms. They watch us from a painted gallery. They half-hide behind painted columns. The lady of the house looks down on us, most suspiciously. One has the eerie sense that they are real and we are the ghosts – from future time.

What Paolo Veronese created inside the villa made art history, and his tricks of perspective continue to surprise and charm the viewer; in fact, the Maser frescoes are probably the only ones in the world which are always greeted with a smile by the viewer, whether venerable art historian or Alpine hillbilly.

This villa, like the Venetian palaces, changed hands as fortunes changed. The penultimate historic figure to become proprietor was Lodovico Manin, Venice's last crowned doge, who died in 1802. The present owners are the heirs of Count Giuseppe Volpi, the industrial magnate who brought electricity to Venice; he also created the nationwide Ciga hotel chain. From his Excelsior Hotel on the Lido he launched, in 1932, the Venice Film Festival. Appropriately, the first film shown was *Grand Hotel*. Volpi was also the creator of Porto Marghera, the area between Venice and Mestre, which brought modern heavy industry and jobs to Venice, and is now held responsible for the industrial pollution of the lagoon. At Volpi's death in 1947, Venice's cardinal-patriarch, Angelo Roncalli, later to become Pope John XXIII, presided; and the press hailed Volpi as 'the last of the Doges'.

The life of Art is long, we are told, and man's life is certainly not. Although Venice may one day vanish beneath the Adriatic, it has lasted a long time, not only as a working city but as a work of art. Although the Venetians produced

St. George killing the Dragon. *Vittore Carpaccio painted this for the Scuola di S. Giorgio degli Schiavoni, the social centre for Venice's large Dalmatian community. The saint, who has now been struck from the books as he never existed, had to slay the dragon because it was too attentive to the princess, seen on the right.*

very little literature (only in this century have they produced a major novelist, P. M. Pasinetti), they have produced an astonishing number of remarkable painters. But then did the painters create the city – which looks like a painting – or did the city influence the painters? Certainly every square looks like a set for an opera that is about to begin.

Hazlitt thought that each art is at its peak at the beginning. This certainly seems to be true of Venetian painting. At the beginning of Venice's prosperity, painters were in great demand: churches, government buildings, even trade union halls wanted their walls illustrated with familiar stories. Painters were regarded by the Venetians with that same mixture of reverence and contempt that we now reserve for film directors. When a major painter revealed his latest work, it was like a film première. Carpaccio was one of the most splendid of proto-movie makers. In the Scuola di S. Giorgio, he painted the story of St. George and the dragon. Here, St. George is played by the Robert Redford of his day, while the dragon is handled by Steven Spielberg's special effects department. Strewn across the ground are the remains of youths and maidens, idly gnawed, the leftovers of the dragon's last supper. There was to be nothing ever again so horrific until our own *Texas Chain-Saw Massacre*.

If Carpaccio was, let us say, the William Wyler of Venetian painting, Tintoretto was the Cecil B. De Mille. Tintoretto, like De Mille, was at his best with crowd scenes and fires. In his portrayal of St. Mark, the saint, in the guise of who else but the marvellous Charlton Heston, swoops down from heaven in order to save from torture a fellow actor. His *Origin of the Milky Way*

Paolo Veronese's The Feast in the House of Levi. *The picture's original title was 'The Last Supper', but the Venetian Inquisition objected to some of the supporting cast included by the artist, so to get past the censors the title was changed. Painted for the refectory of the Dominicans at SS. Giovanni e Paolo, the canvas is filled with the extravagance of sixteenth-century Venetian life, and framed by the currently fashionable Palladian arches.*

illustrates the master's highly unusual theory about the origin of that swash of stars. This kind of science fiction will not appeal to purists like Carl Sagan, but the way in which an entire galaxy emerges from the super-star's breast is a sight to be marvelled at. Certainly, it is great 'box-office'.

For more refined audiences, we have Veronese, the Federico Fellini of his day. After he had decorated Maser, he was asked to paint the Last Supper. But the Inquisition complained about the result. What were all these pets, dwarfs, drunks, German soldiers, doing at Christ's last supper? (This was very much the sort of petulant review that Fellini still gets today.) So Veronese made a number of changes. But when the Inquisition insisted that the highly serious dog at the picture's centre was to be replaced by Mary Magdalene, Veronese refused. Then one of the Inquisitors, plainly inspired, said, 'Well, why don't you change the painting's *title*?', and so it became *The Feast in the House of Levi*. That is how the picture was finally released.

Of all Venetian painters, Giorgione is the strangest and, to me, the most evocative. *The Tempest*, for want of a better title, shows a hot summer day. There is a flash of lightning in the distance. A woman nurses her child, and looks at us. A man walks by, and looks at her. We will never know what it is they know, but looking into her face, we see what she will become when she is old. For next to *The Tempest*, in Venice's Accademia, hangs Giorgione's picture of an old woman. Like the young mother, she looks at us, but now she holds in her hand a sheet of paper with the message: '*Col Tempo*'. 'With time you will be like me'.

The Tempest was once called *The Soldier and the Gypsy*. No one knows what Giorgione himself called the painting or what his private patron, probably Gabriele Vendramin, chose to call it. Twenty-five years after its completion, in 1530, another noble, Marcantonio Michiel, wrote: 'it is a small landscape on canvas with the storm, with the gypsy and the soldier, by the hand of Zorzi [Giorgio] of Castelfranco'. Giorgione, or 'Big George', was the nickname he was given by the Venetians, apparently because he was a huge, jovial fellow, who liked nothing better than playing the lute for friends.

Giorgione was one of the first painters anywhere to be allowed to paint what he pleased, and not what the noble patron or the bishop ordered. This fact, together with Giorgione's improvised style, has given *The Tempest* the handy historic label of being the first 'easel painting' and the picture 'with which painting in the modern sense began'. Recent scrutiny by X-ray and reflettoscope (the latter being one of the Olivetti company's contributions to art scholarship), shows that Giorgione's plans changed after he first took brush in hand. Originally, the cupola surmounted a large tower, but in the final version only the former survives. The soldier, or shepherd, now covers an earlier version of a female nude, bathing her feet. Why, in the sixteenth

Jacopo Tintoretto's St. Mark Freeing a Slave. *The saint plunges from the sky to the aid of one of his worshippers in this, the first canvas of a series depicting scenes from the life of St. Mark. The scene blazes with light. To the left is the bearded figure of Tommaso Rangone, the physician from Ravenna, who was apparently the donor of this painting.*

Jacopo Tintoretto's The Origin of the Milky Way. *Jupiter tricked Juno into nursing the baby Hercules. Some of her divine milk fell to earth and gave birth to the lily. On another occasion, some of the milk spilled heavenward. Baby Hercules may have gone to bed hungry that night but the milk droplets he missed became forever the Milky Way.*

Giorgione's The Tempest.
*Everyone loves a good
mystery, and the 'story'
depicted here has been a
mystery from the start.
Giorgione gave it no title.*

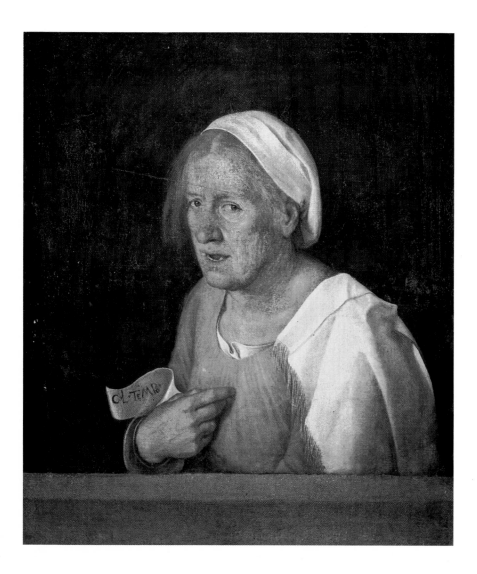

Giorgione's Portrait of an Old Woman. *This small canvas now hangs next to* The Tempest *in the Accademia Gallery in Venice, but the message here is clear. The old woman says it all with the piece of paper in her hand which bears the words 'with time' – you shall be like me.*

century, was the woman referred to as a 'gypsy'? Was it because bathing, or nursing a baby, in the nude was an un-Venetian thing to do? Her stare, is it too unblinking to be that of a local woman? Or is there some somatic feature that identifies her as a gypsy which is lost on today's viewer? The most interesting and never-to-be answered question is what is on the young man's mind? What happens next? (Thunder, surely.) This tiny 'landscape' picture is a perennial teaser – and may 'mean' nothing at all. Walter Pater once said, 'All art constantly aspires towards the condition of music.' Giorgione may have achieved it.

After the great age of painting, and of empire, Venice began to turn inward. With the plague of 1630, human life seemed more than ever fragile. As rulers often do, they called in a commission of thirty-six learned men of medicine, mostly from Padua's famous university. They concluded that there would be no plague. Needless to say, by October the situation was so serious that the Doge announced from St. Mark's pulpit that the Senate had vowed to erect a new church as a sign of thanksgiving to the Virgin Mary when – and if – their prayers for mercy were answered. As it was, during a single November day, 595 people died, and were buried in a common grave.

Now desperate, the Venetians decided to keep their promise to the Madonna even though she had not kept her side of the bargain. The Doge was to lay the cornerstone for the new church on 25 March 1631. But he, too, was ill, and died before the ceremony. Eight days later, a new Doge was inaugurated, but no coronation ceremony could be held because of the plague. Meanwhile, the Senate chose a design for the new church, and a location. It was to be built by Baldassare Longhena near that point of the Dorsoduro where the Customs office still stands. An older church, a small hospital, and some warehouses were torn down to make way for the new church, which was to be supported by perhaps as many as one million wooden pilings driven into the subsoil.

The plague finally ended in mid-November, and the Senate notified all other European powers that Venice's port was to be re-opened. To honour the Madonna for having at last done her part, a temporary wooden church was constructed on the cleared site. On 28 November, a solemn procession made its way across a bridge made of boats, which spanned the Grand Canal from S. Maria del Giglio to the site where S. Maria della Salute was to be built. A ceremony of thanksgiving was held there, as it is still held each year on that date. Other 'plague' churches in Venice include the famous Redentore, built by Palladio on the island of the Giudecca, and those of S. Sebastiano and S. Giobbe, or St. Job, the Old Testament prophet who learned – and taught – a thing or two about human suffering.

Death had concentrated the Venetian mind marvellously well. In Venice's great days the Venetians were accused of worshipping not God, but the State. Now they turned, most seriously, at least for a while, from State to God. An age of religious music had begun, with Gabrielli and Monteverdi. Then came an age of secular music with Vivaldi and Tartini. Charles de Brosses was amazed by the Venetian passion for music. 'Not a single evening goes by', he wrote, 'without a concert somewhere. The people run along the canal to hear it, with such passion that you would suppose that they had never heard anything like it before. You cannot imagine how crazy the city is about this art.'

*The Church of S. Maria
della Salute, designed by
Baldassare Longhena, was
built as a sign of
thanksgiving to the
Madonna for the cessation
of the plague of 1630.*

*The Grand Canal, the
city's main artery, is lined
on each side with the façades
of Venice's many beautiful
palaces, once the private
houses of Venetian merchants.*

What most of us today consider to be 'classical' music began at this time. As the words imply, Italians invented both opera and oratorio, and neither was ever, until this century, for the élite. Every serious town had at least one opera house, and it was usually sold out; the audiences' enthusiasm (or lack thereof) made up for plenty of mediocre performances, rather like village bullfights in Mexico today. Italian composers in the seventeenth and eighteenth centuries were the first to write music for solo voices. In Cremona the Amati family had almost perfected the violin in the sixteenth century and they, with Guarneri and Stradivari, reached a perfection in the next two centuries that was never to be surpassed. Down in Naples, Scarlatti was composing for the harpsichord in the early 1700s, and the Cristofori family in Florence finally invented the pianoforte around 1709. With the violin and the piano available, music left the church, though not entirely, and moved into the concert hall and theatre. Venice was fortunate in having Claudio Monteverdi as a choir director at St. Mark's while Antonio Vivaldi conducted, and wrote for, a local girl's orchestra.

Venice's Ospedale della Pietà, which was behind today's Pietà Church, was not a hospital, but a hostel for orphaned girls. (In other cities, these church-run institutions, sponsored by the government, were also called *conservatori*, which meant poorhouse or orphanage, and which gave us the term 'music conservatory'.) It was there that Vivaldi tried out his new compositions on his captive choir. Since one of his several hundred works is today, if not a jukebox hit, at least a standard Muzak favourite – *The Four Seasons* – it seems appropriate that probably the first audience to hear it in rehearsal was that of the young orphan girls.

Charles de Brosses, who was president of the Burgundy Parliament, visited Venice in 1739. His description of the Pietà orphanage is dated two years before Vivaldi's death:

The girls are educated and maintained at the expense of the State, and their sole training is to excel in music. Thus they sing like angels, and play the violin, flute, organ, oboe, violoncello, and bassoon – in fact, there is no instrument so big as to intimidate them. They are cloistered like nuns. They perform without outside help, and at each concert forty girls take part. I swear there is nothing prettier in the world than to see a young and charming nun, dressed in white, with a spray of pomegranate flowers over her ear, conduct the orchestra and give the beat with all the exactness imaginable.

Some thirty-five years later, the English musician Charles Burney, having seen such a successful organisation, tried to do the same with the Foundling Hospital in London. It was not a feasible idea. Whether this was due to the natural English lack of a musical ear or to the absence of pomegranate flowers in England, we do not know.

VII
CORYATE IN SEVENTEENTH-CENTURY VENICE

*A two-thousand-mile walk from London to the Lagoon
by Thomas Coryate, the first of our Innocents Abroad,
the 'most single-soled, single-souled, and single-shirted Observer',
whose earnest quest also to become England's most gulled traveller
made his a cause for wit among the wittiest men
of Jacobean London.*

THE words 'The Grand Tour' first appeared in letters and in print in the late seventeenth century, but they were not put into upper case or organised until the nineteenth century, when Cook's Tours set forth from Britain. The Germans already had their *wander-jahr*, when young men of means were expected to wander abroad for a year before settling down to the family business, and the business of making a family. Paris, of course, was on their list, perhaps London as well, and both cities were certainly on the lists of the young Italian nobles, who often never visited either Naples or Venice.

Thomas Coryate, if one excludes religious pilgrims and crusaders, must have been the world's first 'crazed tourist'. The son of a clergyman, he attended Winchester and Oxford. In 1608, after a spell of hanging about at the court of King James I, he set out, at the age of thirty, from his native Somerset for France and Italy – on foot. Three years and some 2,000 miles later, he published his impressions as *Coryate's Crudities*. Much of the book was about Venice. Coryate explains why:

I say that had there bin an offer made unto me before I took my journey to Venice, eyther that foure of the richest mannors of Somerset-shire (wherein I was borne) should be gratis bestowed upon me if I never saw Venice, or neither of them if I should see it; although certainly those mannors would do me much good in respect of a state of livelyhood to live in the world, then the sight of Venice: yet notwithstanding I will ever say while I live, that the sight of Venice and her resplendent beauty, antiquities, and monuments, have by many degrees more contented my minde, and satisfied my desires, then those foure Lordshippes could possibly have done.

Carpaccio's The Courtesans. *A study of utter boredom. The ladies are seated on their roof-garden, in their working clothes, and no one rings the door bell, nor does a breeze stir. The young boy (or dwarf?), also dressed in brocade, is their bell-hop. The courtesans' famous elevated clogs are being aired, prior to a promotional stroll through the Piazza. (The clogs were later adopted by noble Venetian ladies but at a height which made them nearly one foot taller, requiring them to walk with a servant on either side to avoid toppling over.)*

Tom's tale of his travels was publicised by him when he returned to London, but he could not find a publisher. So he collected eulogies, or 'blurbs', from everyone he could button-hole. John Donne provided a 'panegyrick' verse of seventy-six lines, plus four other lines in Latin:

> *Oh to what height will love of greatnesse drive*
> *Thy leavened spirit, Sesqui-superlative?*
> *Venice vast lake thou hadst seene, wouldst seeke than*
> *Some vaster thing, and foundst a Cortizan ...*
> *Homely and familiarly, when thou commest backe,*
> *Talke of Will Conqueror, and Prester Jacke.*
> *Goe bashfull man, lest here thou blush to looke*
> *Upon the progress of thy glorious booke ...*
>
> *I think this true;*
> *As Sybils was, your booke is misticall,*
> *For every peece is as much worth as all.*
> *Therefore mine impotency I confesse;*
> *The healths which my braine beares, must be farre less;*
> *Thy Gyant wit o'erthrowes me, I am gone;*
> *And rather then reade all, I would reade none.*

Tom's friend Laurence Whitaker wrote another poetic blurb, dedicated to 'the most peerless Poetical Prose-writer ... and the most singled-soled, single-souled, and single-shirted Observer':

> *Wonder of worlds, that with one fustian case,*
> *One payre of shoes, hast done Ol Odcombe the grace*
> *To make her name knowen past the Alpine hils,*
> *And home return'd hast worne out many quils ....*

Coryate's single pair of shoes was exploited by him to the fullest. At the beginning of the eighteenth century, the original shoes were still hanging in Odcombe Church where his father had been the vicar. Presumably, a mecca for British fetishists. In Coryate's book, he mentions travelling in carriages, and he arrived in Venice by private gondola – not by the common ferry Portia took en route from Padua to Venice, on her mission to mastermind Shylock's trial, and his forced conversion to Christianity. However, Coryate apparently did walk much of the way, there and back, a feat then undertaken only by rare religious pilgrims. Today's 'single-shirters', following in his footsteps with packs on their backs, travel by Euro-rail passes.

Inigo Jones submitted a verse beginning 'Odde is the Combe from whence this Cocke did come, that crowed in Venice', but then takes Tom to task for

A grotesque head on the bell-tower of S. Maria Formosa. This hideous mask is one of the many which were put up on buildings in the seventeenth century. Ruskin found it particularly exciting: 'A head – huge, inhuman, and monstrous – leering in bestial degradation, too foul to be either pictured or described, or to be beheld for more than an instant.'

not tarrying longer in that city. John Chapman commended his book, as does Thomas Campian in a Latin verse. He is compared to Homer, Columbus, Magellan, Drake – it seemed to be a contest among London's literati to praise Tom with tongue in cheek. John Gyfford said,

> *England rejoyce, who now a man hast bred*
> *That is all wit, and learning, save the head.*

And John Pawlet, his neighbour, called him

> *the Man the world doth wonder at.*
> *Whose Braine-pan hath more Pan then Braine by ods,*
> *To make then all Pan with the semi-gods.*

Ben Jonson wrote two blurbs to help the book, and some acrostic verses on the author's name. Coryate for Jonson was 'a great and bold Carpenter of words' but concluded that 'he is so substantive an Author as will stand by himselfe without the need of his Booke to bee joyned with him'. So good an author was he that his book could be done without? With publicity like this, it is a wonder that the book was ever published, but Tom's dedication of the book to the Prince of Wales may have done the trick.

Thomas Coryate sailed from Dover on 14 May 1608, and returned to England on 3 October, Jonson tells us. The author said he spent 'about six weeks in Venice', having passed through Turin, Milan, Cremona, and Padua, encountering for the first time people using a fork when cutting their meat. He does not tell us where he lodged and seldom what he ate, though he marvels at the variety of fruit and vegetables on sale, the frugality of the nobles' tables, and takes a decidedly dim view of Venetian gentlemen doing their own shopping in the public market. He was probably the first Englishman to rail against the gondoliers as being 'the most vicious and licentious varlets' in Venice. But that was the Anglican vicar's son writing, perhaps for parental approval, his beef being that every gondolier in the Rialto tried to hijack foreign male passengers and take them to a courtesan's lair – where, of course, our investigative reporter eventually went on his own two feet, with his famous shoes.

Coryate admired the Doge's new prison ('there is not a fairer prison in all Christendome', he wrote, referring to the architecture) and in mentioning the overhead passage which linked the new building with the Doge's Palace, did not know that his Romantic compatriots 200 years later would dub it 'the Bridge of Sighs'. Like most travel writers, Coryate did not know the language of the country he was writing about, but mentions conversing in Greek with a Greek patriarch after a service in S. Giorgio dei Greci. He inflicts Latin on his readers, as he probably did on the Venetians as well. He had a letter of

introduction to the British ambassador, Sir Henry Wotton, and his writings suggest that he paid court to the knight at his house in 'St. Hieronimo Street', near the Ghetto, where 'in the middest of Popery, superstition, and idolatry, he hath sermons and services after the Protestant manner', adding 'in this street also doth famous Frier Paul dwell'. It is clear that Coryate did not meet Friar Paolo Sarpi, the church reformer, whose fame had reached London. One suspects that, like most foreign travellers, Coryate sought out the company of his own people. His impressions of Sarpi the man could have been most interesting.

Recovered from his first fork, Tom next saw, again for the first time, women acting on the stage; and he found that they performed 'with as good a grace, action, gesture, and whatsoever convenient for a Player, as ever I saw any masculine Actor'. He also saw his first courtesans at the theatre, but they were masked and veiled, so his curiosity was not yet satisfied. On Murano, he ate his first clams, calling them the best, but smallest, oysters he had eaten.

He visited the Scuola di S. Rocco and admired the music, and the 'beautified walls [decorated] with sundry delicate pictures'; he tells us that the *scuola*'s yearly revenue amounted to 6,094 pounds, 16 shillings and 8 pence – but not a word about Tintoretto's *Crucifixion*. The picture Tom most admired in Venice was a painting of a leg of veal. Was he short of funds and hungry? The Venetians excelled in 'manual arts', in Coryate's opinion.

Coryate was also attracted to the Ospedale della Pietà, though he mentions no music:

If any Venetian courtesan happens to have any children (as indeed they have but a few, for according to the old proverb the best carpenters make the fewest chips), they are brought up either at their own charge or in a certain house of the city appointed for no other use but only for the bringing up of the courtesans' bastards, which I saw eastward above St. Mark's street near to the seaside. In the south wall of which building that looketh towards the sea, I observed a certain iron gate inserted into a hollow piece of the wall, betwixt which grate and plain stone beneath it there is a convenient little space to put in an infant. Hither doth the mother or somebody for her bring the child shortly after it is born into the world. If the body of it be no greater but that it may conveniently without any hurt to the infant be conveighed in at the aforesaid space, they put it there without speaking at all to anybody who is in the house to take charge thereof. From thenceforth the mother is absolutely discharged of her child. But if the child be grown to that bigness that they cannot conveigh it through that space, it is carried back again to the mother.

In St. Mark's Square, he took in a little torturing – two men had been hoisted up between the columns in the Piazzetta, their 'joynts ... for the time loosed and pulled asunder'. He also, worse, saw men kissing each other on the

The tilting bell-tower of the Church of S. Giorgio dei Greci, the Orthodox church built by Venice's once large Greek community. The view is looking towards the Grand Canal.

cheek in greeting; equally 'uncivill and unseemely' were the women who went about the square topless; 'almost all the wives, widowes and mayds do walke abroad with their breasts all naked, and many of them have their backes also naked even almost to the middle'. Tom would seem to have had another 'exclusive' story here, and, though perhaps unaware of it, he was moving closer to perdition. The intrepid and thorough chronicler was steeling himself to deal with the courtesans, for the gentle reader's sake.

Coryate's figure for the courtesan population is nearly double the already astounding figure given by Marino Sanudo. Tom records 20,000 in Venice, but admittedly he was including the smaller islands of Murano and Malamocco. The Venetians, he warns, should have been in fear lest 'their winking at such uncleannesse should be an occasion to draw down upon them God's curse and vengeance from heaven, and to consume their city with fire and brimstone'. But the Venetians, according to Tom, thought that their wives' chastity was preserved by the presence of the courtesans and he noted that the nobles' wives were never seen abroad. A gentlewoman was seen in public only at great weddings, 'or at the Christning of a Jew, or late in the evening rowing in a gondola'.

Tom's research into the courtesan problem informed him that if a client cunningly escaped without payment, 'she will either cause thy throate to be cut by her Ruffiano if he can catch thee in the city, or procure thee to be arrested and clapped in prison'. As he warmed to his subject, Tom wrote: 'in the courtesan's cheekes thou shalt see the Lilly and the Rose strive for supremacy ... thou shalt see her decked in many chaines of gold and orient pearls like a second Cleopatra ... thou wilt say with the wiseman, and that very truely, that they are like a golden ring in a swines snowt....' The courtesan made 'heart-tempting harmony of her voice' and was 'a good Rhetorician and most elegant discourser'. He added that she kept a picture of the Virgin Mary by her bedside, but then he gave the game away.

Thus have I described unto thee the Venetian Courtesans; but because I have related so many particulars of them, as few Englishmen that have lived many yeares in Venice, can do the like, or at the least if they can, they will not upon their returne into England, I beleeve thou wilt cast an aspersion of wantonnesse upon me, and say I could not know all these matters without mine owne experience. I answere thee, that although I might have knowne them without my experience, yet for my better satisfaction, I went to one of their noble houses (I will confesse) to see the manner of their life, and observe their behaviour ... I both wished the conversion of the Cortesan that I saw, and did my endevour by perswasive termes to convert her ... So did I visite the noble Cortezan, view her own amorous person, heare her talke, observe her fashion of life, and yet was nothing contaminated therewith, nor corrupted in manner ... I have at large deciphered and as it were anatomized a Venetian Cortesan unto thee, as though wouldest have me of thy selfe upon the like request.

As someone once said, there'll always be an England.

Coryate in his *Crudities* mentions with pride that his king's portrait hung in a place of honour in the Doge's Palace, along with that of Philip II of Spain, and 'the pictures of the rest of the Dukes to Marino Grimanno, which was the immediate predecessor to this present Duke Leonardo Donato'. That is the only reference to Doge Leonardo Donà (Donato being the Latinised version of his name), which can only mean that Coryate never met him, for he was the second most important figure in Venice of that time. The British ambassador could have arranged a meeting, for many doges actually enjoyed taking foreign visitors on sightseeing tours of the city, one of the occasions when they could justify going about without the pomp of State.

Leonardo Donà became doge in 1606, in his sixty-ninth year. Donà is still remembered to history as the doge who hired Friar Paolo Sarpi to be his personal theologian and adviser. His predecessor, Doge Marino Grimani, had greatly angered the Pope by ordering the arrest of two Venetian priests charged with common crimes. The Pope wanted them extradited to the papal states for trial; this pleased neither the Venetian Senate nor the people, and Donà's election, after twenty-two ballots, was probably due to the fact that he was not known to be a papal enthusiast.

The Donà family had its palace in the S. Stio parish, but when Leonardo was born most of the wealth was gone. He served the Republic first as bailiff in Constantinople, and then as *podestà* at Brescia in Lombardy. A *podestà* was not only a mayor but also sheriff; and Donà set about ridding Brescia of the brigands then infesting the outskirts. He was later posted to Rome, as Venetian ambassador. Pope Sixtus V was so impressed by his abilities that he gave him a knighthood and eventually offered the unmarried and unordained Donà the cardinal's red hat if the former sheriff would take over the bishop's throne in Brescia. Donà refused, by quoting the Gospel, not then a fashionable thing to do in Rome: '*Manete in vocatione qua vocati estis*', or, roughly, 'no square pegs in round holes'. One of the most powerful men in Rome, Cardinal Camillo Borghese (later Pope Paul V), reportedly groused one day to Ambassador Donà that the Venetians were altogether too independent in their thinking and acting, adding 'If I were pope, I would excommunicate them all!' to which the ambassador replied: 'If I were Doge, I would laugh at the excommunication!' The story seems too prophetic to be true; but the point was well-taken and Donà's own personality revealed.

Donà knew as well as anyone the sorry state of financial affairs in Venice when he was crowned doge. He did not throw silver coins to the people as his predecessor had done, nor did he give them free wine and cakes. The people took that as a bad omen and, indeed, bad news arrived three months later. Pope Paul V himself gave Venice twenty-four days to release the two priests

The Palazzo Sanudo Van-Axel. Built in the 1470s, this palace is the only one in Venice with the original wooden door and knocker.

from prison, or else the entire Republic would be anathematised. Friar Sarpi was consulted. In Venice, he maintained, the pope had spiritual but not temporal power. A manifesto was issued declaring the papal edict to be 'null and void of value', and the Doge ordered all churches to remain open and masses to be said. The Jesuits decided that things were getting too hot; they fled Venice. The next year, the French ambassador in Venice persuaded the Pope and the Doge to make peace, but Rome was not pleased when the Senate then ruled that the Jesuits, the pope's soldiers, could not return to Venetian territory. Seven months later, Friar Sarpi was set upon and stabbed thrice in the neck by assassins from the mainland. He surprised everyone by surviving and later commented, 'I recognised the stylus of the Roman Curia' – a triple play on the Latin, as 'stylus' means writing-pen, style, and the stiletto dagger.

The Venice described by Coryate was also plagued by pirates, but he seemed to be unaware of that form of terrorism on the high seas. When Donà took office, all Venice's merchant ships had to carry eighteen guns, six six-pounder cannons, and four twelve-pounder cannons, as well as eight mortars. The last were used for hurtling boulders at the small, eight-oared pirate ships. Maritime insurance had been a source of Venetian revenue when the premium was between two and six per cent of the cargo's value. Now, because of piracy routinely being practised by English and Dutch merchant ships, the insurance premiums rose to forty per cent and the insurance business was wrecked.

Doge Donà's worst pirate adversaries, however, came inexplicably from a small fishing port called Segna, in what is now Yugoslavia. The Segna pirates would dash out to attack and rob the Venetian galleys, then flee to hidden coves before the mighty cannons could be turned on them. These pirates had the curious name of Uskoks, and the even more curious habit of giving one-tenth of their stolen booty to their bishop. The tithing so excited the church that they wanted more, and so Segna's Franciscan and Domenican friars would often join the pirate expeditions, like so many jolly, sea-going Friar Tucks. These Illyrian *mafiosi* could justify their thieving by saying that the merchandise was being exported to Moslem 'infidels' or, if that rang hollow, that the shippers were 'Jews'.

So adept were these Uskoks that Pope Sixtus asked them to send him 2,000 slaves to man his galleys at the papal port of Ancona. For some time, Venice also suffered from the fact that the cream of her young nobles no longer felt it their duty to go to sea and become captains. The Senate, which set the wages aboard the ships, had also failed to keep pace with inflation. A galley setting sail from Venice was likely to have only about 50 paid freemen manning the oars, rowing next to 140 convicts serving sentences of hard labour.

Unlike the pope and the Knights of Malta – in Venice the latter were called 'pirates parading with crosses' – the Venetians never resorted to slave labour on their ships. Perhaps that, or conscription, would have helped the Republic as the Venetian sailors and oarsmen, in a 1605 report, were described as being 'worthless and unscrupulous creatures, so that when attacked by pirates they not only help them, but take to plundering themselves'.

Leonardo Donà was aware of this sorry state of affairs when he was elected doge, which may explain the sobriety of his coronation. He knew he would be presiding over the melancholy decline of the Republic.

While Friar Sarpi's history of the Council of Trent was being read and admired in its pseudonymous London edition (unlike Coryate he rapidly found a publisher), Doge Donà began to fail in health. Venice's papalist families exaggerated his condition; there was even a rumour of his death. When the Doge appeared at a public ceremony, the people, still sulky at not getting coronation cake, began shouting 'Bring back the Doge Grimani – the friend of the poor!' Donà decided to make no more public appearances. He died in 1612 and was buried in S. Giorgio Maggiore, which had been completed two years earlier, on the island distanced from the rabble.

Although Thomas Coryate's *Crudities* ignored all the crude political facts of Venetian life, his social impressions are easily the funniest ever written, equalled only in our time by the broodings of Miss Lorelei Lee, in Anita Loos's *Gentlemen Prefer Blondes*. Tom and Lorelei have in common a wide-eyed innocence and an unintentional wittiness which only a comic genius could have produced. We know who created the 1920s blonde American flapper, but who really created the character called Thomas Coryate? Plainly, he is too good to be true, and therefore the suspicion of 'forgery' arises, just as it did a few years ago when a Rome scuba diver accidentally found in the sea the two magnificent 'Riace Bronzes' – Greek statues from the fifth century BC, probably by Phidias. They are too perfect, and the Coryate in the *Crudities* is the too-perfect fool, as well as being the wisest of observers.

Coryate's description of the Venetian courtesans, 'these amorous Calypsoes, these elegant discoursers', may not have started a stampede to Venice, but almost everyone, including Montaigne, came to the city to satisfy his own curiosity. They were definitely an asset to the tourist trade, as later was the Venetian Carnival, and the Ridotto gambling casino. The serious male tourist could look at painted Madonnas by day and at painted courtesans by night. Sometimes he must have had a sense of *déjà vu* in the evening: the ladies of the night were sometimes models for painters by day. Eventually the courtesans were banned, even though the taxes they paid had launched many a Venetian galley. A clerically-inspired Puritan drive put an end to their reign; coincidentally, the government, always practical, had discovered that increased, 'cleaner' revenue could be had from the gambling tables, and from Carnival. The final act of Venice's decadence was about to be staged.

VIII

CARNIVAL AND DECLINE

By the eighteenth century,
another passion was raging in Venice – gambling.
The city was filled with private gambling dens, like the
famous Il Ridotto. Fortunes were made at dice and cards, but,
mostly, fortunes were lost. All classes of people mingled in these
small rooms where the law required that all except patricians be
masked. Palaces which had been conceived as trade centres, as
corporate headquarters, were now dedicated not to business,
but to the relentless pursuit of pleasure.

T HE same Doge who led the solemn procession to inaugurate the temporary church of the Salute, seven years later granted to Marco Dandolo a gambling concession in his palace next to the S. Moisé church. It was set in what Dandolo called '*il ridotto*' (literally, 'reduced quarters'), the foyer of his palace, to be entered from a side street. It was almost certainly the first time that a patrician palace had been opened for gambling anywhere in Europe. It soon became famous all over the Continent, and Dandolo's 'reduced quarters' reduced many a European family fortune. It also reaped money for the Venetian treasury, which was by then in a sorry state from so many wars won and lost, so many dominions gone.

In the middle of the seventeenth century, the Book of Gold (shut forever as of 1297) was re-opened – for more gold. The nobles listed in that book protested. They knew better than anyone the true value of a noble title. But the Senate and the Great Council agreed to admit new names, upon application and after due investigation. The one real requirement, however, was 100,000 gold ducats (about one million dollars today) to be paid to the treasury. A number of wealthy Venetians eagerly paid to be admitted to the Book of Gold, not so much for a title (there are no hereditary titles in a republic), but to be able to take part in the governing of the city.

It was highly appropriate, like so many other things that have happened in Venice, that the Doge who presided over Venice's entry into the eighteenth

The Ridotto, formerly the 'reduced quarters' within
the Palazzo Dandolo, where the family probably lived
during the colder months to avoid heating the entire
palace. When the Government decided to allow
Venice's first gambling casino, it was to the Ridotto
that Venetians and foreigners alike flocked to augment
the Republic's treasury. Today it is a theatre.

A Dutch sea captain, the P. T. Barnum of his day, brought this rhinoceros to Europe in 1741. Ten years later it arrived in Venice for the Carnival and everyone turned out to see the freakish sight. Nobleman Girolamo Mocenigo commissioned Pietro Longhi to paint the animal, the result being almost as successful as the rhino itself. Longhi, like other painters, made several copies, and his pupils made even more. The rhino's Christian name is not recorded, but perhaps that practice only came in with Barnum.

century, Silvestro Valier, had bought his way into the Book of Gold when he was only nineteen, at the bargain price of 20,500 ducats. But then he was a successful gambling man. Now ennobled, he could take off his mask when going to the Ridotto with his wealthy wife, Elisabetta Querini. He was elected doge, according to a contemporary report, 'because he was decorative', which was, by then, as good a reason as any. When the Infanta of Spain passed through Venice on her way to marry Emperor Leopold I, she was welcomed by Doge Valier, who wore a cloth-of-gold robe, lined with small diamonds. She made him a knight on the spot; and presented him with a large diamond, which the Senate allowed him to keep. Gone were the days when the doge could only accept sweetmeats and scented balms. Valier also insisted that his wife should have her own coronation, even though that ceremony had been outlawed fifty years earlier. When Russia's Peter the Great came to Venice in 1698, he was astounded at the opulence of the Doge's court. And its frivolity: at all times, Valier carried a deck of cards – just in case. He is buried in the most delirious of Baroque tombs in the Church of SS. Giovanni e Paolo, the deck of cards no doubt tucked in his shroud.

Venice was now ready to sacrifice publicness for privateness, or call it Duty for Pleasure. The Venetians have always been secretive about themselves – as today's local tax inspectors can, or hope to, verify. Only one Venetian ever told All. He was Giacomo Casanova, who wrote Venice's only proper, improper memoir.

It is curious that of the three million Venetians who ever lived, only two, if you don't count artists, are known to all the world: one is Marco Polo, who travelled to China and back again; the other is Casanova, who travelled to many beds and back again. Thanks to his memoirs, he is known to the world as a great lover. Actually he was his century's most brilliant authority on taxes; he was also far too much of an Enlightened free-thinker for conservative Venice.

But in the age of Rousseau and Voltaire and Jefferson, Venice was no longer relevant, except as an artifact. Yet it still had a form of government that intrigued the thinkers of the so-called Age of Reason. As the Venetian Republic was drawing to a close, the American Republic was being born.

'We hold these Truths to be self-evident, that all Men are created equal, that they are endowed by their Creator with certain unalienable rights, that among these are Life, Liberty, and the Pursuit of Happiness', wrote the Americans when they declared themselves to be independent of British rule in 1776, twenty-one years before the fall of the world's longest-lived republic. The men who wrote those noble words, and who devised the Constitution of the United States, were members of a well-to-do, sometimes wealthy, land-owning élite. Had the original thirteen American colonies been settled

Human beings have always needed to transcend the ordinary. In Venice, people can still escape their everyday lives – through fantasy and masks.

somehow in Venice, rather than in Virginia, those men would have been members of the Great Council. They, too, may have thought that their sort would go on running their country for ever, and were certainly not prepared even to entertain the notion of giving the vote to people without property.

The idea that one of mankind's God-given rights could also include 'the Pursuit of Happiness' is the one 'revolutionary' idea in the Declaration. And in 1776, Venetians were pursuing just that, relentlessly. The rest of Europe pretended to be shocked by the fact that Venice had decided that its Carnival, once intended to last the traditional three weeks preceding Lent, should now go on for six months of the year. And shocked Europeans, if they could scrape up the money, headed straight for Venice to join in the fun. Moralistic commentators have ascribed the Republic's collapse to Venetian wantonness, almost certainly exaggerated by visitors returning home, like soldiers returning to barracks, boasting of sexual adventures. But this is rather as if the Roaring Twenties, and bobbed hair, had caused the 1929 Crash and the 1930s Depression. Maybe – who knows? – the Venetian élite had read America's Declaration of Independence. They had life, they had liberty, and for

With the revival of the modern Carnival, Venetian mask-makers are everywhere. Many of the masks are designed not to be worn but to hang on one's walls, like antlers.

*Today's Venetians
celebrate Carnival with
music, with dancing and
with costumes.*

The object is to see, but not be seen. To suspect, but not to know. Mystery, anonymity, ambiguity.

happiness and its pursuit, they read licentiousness.

The American Founding Fathers were fascinated by the longevity and apparent solvency of the Venetian Republic. In the Venetian archives there is the first communication from the new American Republic to the almost one-thousand-year-old Venetian Republic. It is dated 1784, and it begins: 'The United States of America in Congress assembled, judging that an intercourse between the said United States and The Most Serene Republic of Venice, founded on the principles of equality, reciprocity and friendship, may be of mutual advantage, on the 12th day of May, has issued the commission . . .' and so on.

The three American commissioners were writing from Paris. They requested good relations between the two countries, and, naturally, trade. The signatures on this document are first, John Adams, second, Benjamin Franklin and third, Thomas Jefferson. The Venetian ambassador in Paris made a translation before sending the letter to Venice. Unfortunately, he had the same trouble that most Americans had with the handwriting of Thomas Jefferson whose name, in Italian, became John Jesternon.

Interestingly enough, John Jesternon so admired the works of the Venetian architect, Palladio, that he imitated him when he built Monticello, his house in Virginia. Jefferson, like many other professional or amateur architects who took inspiration from Palladio, never saw any of the Venetian master's buildings. There was no need to. Palladio published in Venice in 1570 his own *Four Books of Architecture* (usually translated as *The Four Orders*). They were later published in almost every European language; and these books immensely influenced Western architecture throughout the next century. Inigo Jones (who *did* come to Venice) was the first major British architect to be influenced by the Palladian style. Christopher Wren soon followed, and when the Earl of Burlington's house in Piccadilly was remodelled, it emerged as Palladian. Burlington's country house at Chiswick is, like Jefferson's Monticello, a fair copy of Palladio's villa, 'La Rotonda'. But unlike Monticello (built in a southern latitude), Chiswick's four elegant porches are calculated to chill even the most socially ambitious house-guest – no warm Italian breeze for him. With characteristic compassion, Alexander Pope expressed his pity for the English victims of the Palladian mania:

> *They clap four slices of pilaster on't,*
> *That, lac'd with bits of rustic, makes a front*
> *Shall call the winds through long arcades to roar,*
> *Proud to catch cold at a Venetian door;*
> *Conscious they act a true Palladian part,*
> *And if they starve, they starve by rules of art.*

Other London buildings which followed the Palladian order were the Horse Guards, St. Martin's-in-the-Fields, the Banqueting Hall in Whitehall, and the terraces of Regent's Park. In America, public or private buildings which are either eighteenth-century, or look as if they belong in Washington, DC, are children, sometimes bastards, of the Palladian school.

But the Venetian Republic itself was no longer a good model for an American, or for any other Republic. With loss of power, the State became ever more paranoid. Citizens were constantly being accused, and sometimes convicted, of un-Venetian activities. The archives hold all the Inquisition's files, including the ledger for the year 1775. On the left-hand side the Inquisitors noted the crime; then, on the right-hand side, they wrote the sentence. Giacomo Casanova was found guilty of acts against the holy religion – he had introduced two young noblemen to freemasonry. The Inquisition found Casanova guilty, and sentenced him to five years in prison in the wooden cells beneath the lead-plated roof of the Doge's Palace – the *piombi*.

Every nineteenth-century visitor came to see Casanova's cell and Lord Byron, who wanted no romantic legend to die, reportedly spent an entire day re-carving the graffiti on the cell walls which were being worn away by the touch of admiring fingers. When Balzac saw Casanova's cell he said, all in all, he had seen fashionable apartments in Paris that were a lot worse.

Casanova escaped from the prison after two years, and a Venetian clerk describes in these archives how he, and another prisoner, a priest, escaped over the roof of the building. The Inquisitors held the prison warden responsible, and he was promptly sentenced to ten years in his own prison. Unlike Casanova, he was not sent to the cells under the roof, but down to the dungeons. Casanova's own account of his escape in 1756 is one of the most exciting stories in literature, a real cliff-hanger – or even drainpipe-hanger.

. . . it was just as the clock was striking midnight on the 31st of October that I escaped from my cell, as the reader will soon see. . . .

At eight o'clock without needing any help, my opening was made. I had broken up the beams, and the space was twice the size required. I got the plate of lead off in one piece. I could not do it by myself, because it was riveted. The monk came to my aid, and by dint of driving the bar between the gutter and the lead I succeeded in loosening it, and then, heaving at it with our shoulders, we beat it up till the opening was wide enough. On putting my head out through the hole I was distressed to see the brilliant light of the crescent moon then entering on its first quarter. This was a piece of bad luck which must be borne patiently, and we should have to wait till midnight, when the moon would have gone to light up the Antipodes. On such a fine night as this everybody would be walking in St. Mark's Place, and I dared not show myself on the roof as the moonlight would have thrown a huge shadow of me on the place, and have drawn towards me all

Most of the festivities took place originally in private houses, but now they are centred on St. Mark's Square.

eyes, especially those of Messer-Grande *and his myrmidons, and our fine scheme would have been brought to nothing by their detestable activity. I immediately decided that we could not escape till after the moon set; in the meantime I prayed for the help of God, but did not ask Him to work any miracles for me . . .*

Our time had come. The moon had set. I hung half of the ropes by Father Balbi's neck on one side and his clothes on the other. I did the same to myself, and with our hats on and our coats off we went to the opening.

I got out the first, and Father Balbi followed me. . . Keeping on my hands and knees, and grasping my pike firmly I pushed it obliquely between the joining of the plates of lead, and then holding the side of the plate which I had lifted I succeeded in drawing myself up to the summit of the roof. The monk had taken hold of my waistband to follow me, and thus I was like a beast of burden who has to carry and draw along at the same time; and this on a steep and slippery roof. . .

My eye caught a window on the canal side, and two-thirds of the distance from the gutter to the summit of the roof. It was a good distance from the spot I had set out from, so I concluded that the garret lighted by it did not form part of the prison I had just broken. It could only light a loft, inhabited or uninhabited, above some rooms in the palace, the doors of which would probably be opened by daybreak. I was morally sure that if the palace servants saw us they would help us to escape, and not deliver us over to the Inquisitors, even if they had recognised us as criminals of the deepest dye; so heartily was the State Inquisition hated by everyone.

It was thus necessary for me to get in front of the window, and letting myself slide softly down in a straight line I soon found myself astride on top of the dormer-roof. Then grasping the sides I stretched my head over, and succeeded in seeing and touching a small grating, behind which was a window of square panes of glass joined with thin strips of lead. I did not trouble myself about the window, but the grating, small as it was, appeared an insurmountable difficulty, failing a file, and I had only my pike.

Philosophic reader, if you will place yourself for a moment in my position, if you will share the sufferings which for fifteen months had been my lot, if you think of my danger on the top of a roof, where the slightest step in a wrong direction would have cost me my life, if you consider the few hours at my disposal to overcome difficulties which might spring up at any moment, the candid confession I am about to make will not lower me in your esteem; at any rate, if you do not forget that a man in an anxious and dangerous position is in reality only half himself.

It was the clock of St. Mark's striking midnight, which, by a violent shock, drew me out of the state of perplexity I had fallen into. The clock reminded me that the day just beginning was All Saints' Day – the day of my patron saint (at least if I had one) . . . The chime seemed to me a speaking talisman, commanding me to be up and doing, and promising me the victory. Lying on my belly I stretched my head down towards the grating, and pushing my pike into the sash which held it I resolved to take it out in a piece. In a quarter of an hour I succeeded, and held the whole grate in my hands, and putting it on one side I easily broke the glass window, though wounding my left hand. In an instant I was over the parapet as far as my chest, sustained only by my elbows.

I shudder still when I think of this awful moment, which cannot be conceived in all its horror. My natural instinct made me almost unconsciously strain every nerve to regain the parapet, and — I had nearly said miraculously — I succeeded.

The Roman Catholic church in Europe has always taken a particularly black view of freemasonry, ever since it crossed the Channel from its native England. No ruler, and the pope was a temporal as well as spiritual ruler, has ever liked the idea of a secret society, or even one with secrets, in its midst. Even though an élite group like the masons, for whom Casanova was caught recruiting, swore allegiance to God, in his role as the great Architect of the Universe, they could still be plotting something, somewhere, against God's only authorised church. Certainly, in France, the freemasons were indeed anti-clerical, as those who favoured common justice tended to be. Although this was rarely the case in other countries, the French example was enough to make nervous prelates blame the masons for their temporal setbacks. As it turned out, their paranoia was not unjustified. In the second half of the last century, the Risorgimento (the romantic name given to the unification

The door to Giacomo Casanova's prison cell on the top floor of the Doge's Palace from where, aided and hindered by a priest who was also a prisoner, he managed a dramatic escape. The wooden cell was roomy by contemporary prison standards, but it was uncomfortably hot when the sun warmed the roof's lead shingles. The ceiling was also too low for the six-feet-tall writer, musician, con-man and confidante of European sovreigns and the Pope. Casanova also missed mixed company, so he carried out the best-chronicled jail-break in history.

The Bucintoro Returning to the Quay on Ascension Day by Canaletto. The Doge ordered all Venetian gondolas to be painted black, but for ceremonial duties such as the Wedding of the Sea ritual on Ascension Day, the Bucintoro was brought out of the Arsenal for his transport. No Mississippi showboat was ever a grander sight.

movement that finally stripped the pope of his temporal rule over Rome, and unified Italy as a single nation) was led almost entirely by freemasons, and the general who commanded the proto-Italian troops, Giuseppe Garibaldi, was at one time the Grand Master of Italy's masons.

At least half of the American presidents have been masons, and all male British sovereigns and their brothers have been masons. But in the eighteenth century Catholic rulers, like the Pope, benign despot though he may have been, saw enemies of the Establishment everywhere. When Giacomo Casanova was working as a paid informer of the Venetian Inquisition, he had the savvy to warn the Three Inquisitors that they should not allow in Venice a coming theatrical show based on the story of Coriolanus, a story whose implications the Three might not yet have grasped.

By the eighteenth century Venice was a shell, a bejewelled shell, of the world power that she once had been. The Carnival was now an almost all-year-round event. People came from every part of the world to Venice, to dress up, to wear masks, to gamble, to fall in love – if not with Venice, with themselves. And they still do.

Carnem levare, as it was called in Latin, was the Christian's last fling before Lent. In the fourteenth century, there was a carnival in Florence, in Rome, and in Nice. During the next century, the Venetian version came into being and, typically, had to be different. The Council of Ten had already given permission for Venetian youths to form social clubs, called the *Compagnie de Calza* – 'the Stocking Companions'. Members of one club would be identified by their yellow leg-stockings, while a rival club would wear red hose. The stocking boys were well-heeled to boot, as the simple Venetian could not afford such silken finery. After the clubs wearied of challenging one another to the usual boat race, they began competing in masked balls on *Martedì Grasso*, the day before Ash Wednesday. The Venetian Carnival evolved from those clubs. If the Blue Stocking Club had existed then, and had refused to take part, we would know that sombre phrase's origin was Venetian.

The Feastday of St. Roch *by Canaletto. Were it not for this delightful crowd scene set against the backdrop of the* scuola, *most people probably would not recall this façade, the work of three architects during the first half of the sixteenth century. Once Venice's richest club house had been built, the board of directors accepted bids from artists to decorate the interior. By a clever ruse, the young, ultra-modern Jacopo Tintoretto won the competition – though one board member offered to increase his financial contribution if Tintoretto was dropped for a more traditional painter. Today, his cycle of fifty-six paintings in the* scuola *is the reason for its fame.*

*La Fenice, Venice's only remaining opera house.
Inaugurated in 1792, the interior was completely
rebuilt after a fire in 1831 (*la fenice *means
'phoenix'). It remains one of the best examples of the
special requirements of Venetian building, its well-
integrated appearance belying its irregular site. This
beautiful theatre is also famous for staging the world
première of Verdi's* La Traviata, *which was a
resounding flop. Too modern, perhaps.*

After the Council of Trent, which was the Vatican's answer to the Protestant Reformation, Venice curtailed its Carnival. Later, in good times, Carnival made a comeback. Most of the festivities were in private houses, not in the Square. Under fascism, the wearing of masks in public was illegal, since behind the mask could lurk an anti-fascist subversive or even an anarchist. In the 1950s, a rich South American named Carlos de Beistegui, tried single-handedly (the other hand held a bag of American gold) to re-launch Venice's Carnival 'among men of good taste and culture ... so that Venice shall become the university and laboratory of Free Time and Carnevale'. He bought the ruined Labia Palace and restored it; he invited the likes of Maria Callas, Elsa Maxwell, and others, to come to a masked ball. A group of Venice parish priests and left wing layabouts organised demonstrations against the rich foreigner, and he soon fled the city, disguised, some say, as a friar. It was a rare – perhaps unique – example of Venetians allowing money of any kind to get away from them. But the Labia Palace remained beautifully restored, with its Tiepolo ceilings, depicting Antony and Cleopatra.

Human beings have always needed to transcend the ordinary. That is why people still escape their everyday lives in Venice – through fantasy and masks and mirrors. Better bad poetry than dull truth. Certainly they will never find anywhere else anything quite like the Venetian Carnival – or *Carne-Vale* – which means 'flesh farewell'. After one last riotous feast follow the forty days of Lent, forty days of austerity when no flesh may be devoured. Today's Venetians, or would-be Venetians, say goodbye to the flesh for three whole weeks, to the immense joy of the Ministry of Tourism. They celebrate with music, with dancing, with costumes – and with masks. The object is to see but not be seen. To suspect but not to know. Mystery, ambiguity, anonymity. And, theoretically, *anything* goes.

IX

VENICE AND
THE ROMANTICS

*When the Venetian Republic was abolished by Napoleon
Bonaparte in 1797, the Most Serene Republic serenely expired,
and that was the end of Venice as a great capital. The city became
a part of Austria at the beginning of the Romantic Century –
the 1800s. During that century just about every romantic
or would-be romantic figure came to
delight in Venice.*

NAPOLEON just walked into Venice. Not literally, of course, since the
causeway from the mainland was not built until 1844, and he himself
did not turn up until 1807, for a week's working holiday. In 1797, the
fame of the 28-year-old Corsican was such that Venice, by now bankrupt and
world-weary, may have thought it good business to jump on the Liberty
Bandwagon rolling across Europe, courtesy of the currently fashionable
French Revolution. Although the Venetians had been independent longer
than any other people in the world, they welcomed the little dictator who had
said 'I shall be a second Attila to Venice'. True, in part, to his word, he razed to
the ground some eighty Venetian churches and about forty palaces. A Tree of
Liberty was raised in the Piazza, and a great bonfire was lit. The first thing to
be thrown on the fire was the Book of Gold. But the Venetians are a shrewd
and secretive people. They burned another book. They hid the Book of Gold.
As for the thousand-year-old Republic, it ended when the 120th Doge
removed the doge's hat and gave it to his valet, remarking 'I suppose I won't
be needing this anymore'. Napoleon then gave Venice to Austria, delighting
neither.

History's next bandwagon was called National Unification. This one was
pulled by horses named Patriotism, Sentimentalism, and Copy-cat. For at
least one disinterested observer, the late nineteenth-century political unification of the Italian peninsula was a mistake for all the Italian regions. Needless
to say, there was dancing in St. Mark's Square, as Venice rid itself of the

*The view across to the
island of S. Giorgio
Maggiore, with a mooring
lantern in the foreground.*

*The Palazzo Barbaro,
where Henry James lived
during one of his several
spells in Venice, and
where he set some scenes of*
The Wings of the Dove.
*These rooms were also
frequented by such illustrious
figures as Robert Browning,
John Singer Sargent
and Claude Monet.*

This relief of the Madonna and Child resides in the courtyard of the Palazzo Barbaro.

Austrian 'tyranny' (actually, the Habsburg arrangement was Europe's most enlightened, as it was Europe's least competent). Venice handed itself over to the grab-bag of politicians assembled, or about to assemble, in Rome. Regardless of geographical distance, Venice is always closer to Vienna than to Rome.

The nineteenth century was the first, consciously, to develop and cultivate a sense of the past. The cult of old things was everywhere the rage, and what was older and more picturesque than Venice? Charles Dickens arrived here at night. The next morning when he looked out the window of the Hotel Danieli he said, inventive as always: 'No words can describe the freshness of the air . . . the sparkling of the water under the rays of the sun that shines in the clear blue sky. . . .' You can tell that Dickens was paid handsomely by the word, and no word ever failed him. But what Dickens saw and felt, people still think they see and feel in Venice.

Certainly, Venice was the perfect setting for what Mario Praz referred to as 'The Romantic Agony', while Henry James thought Venice 'the repository of consolations', an ideal place for someone with a broken heart, or someone looking for a heart to break. The most romantic figure of the century, Lord Byron (himself more satirist than romantic) wrote a good deal of his poem, *Don Juan*, in the Mocenigo Palace, between long rovings into the night, searching for girls.

Robert Browning was the most sturdy survivor of a most tiring, but totally romantic, attachment to a lady who expressed the Romantic spirit in a line: 'I shall but love thee better after death'. Browning buried his wife, Elizabeth Barrett, in Florence; then he returned to Venice in 1889 for the last months of his own life because their son and his rich American wife had bought the vast, magnificent Palazzo Rezzonico on the Grand Canal, which Browning sweetly called 'a corner for my old age'.

There have always been 'pop stars'. According to graffiti, even Roman gladiators had their fans. For centuries, musicians, actors, athletes, poets, all have attracted crowds. Lord Byron affected to resent his; and hinted darkly that he was too much gazed upon in England (particularly by Lady Byron), and was happier in Italy, particularly Venice, where he arrived in 1816. He moved into one of the Mocenigo palaces on the Grand Canal, with fourteen servants. Like so many solitary romantic poets, he loved company. But English visitors sometimes overdid it. When Byron and Shelley went horseback riding on the deserted Lido, Byron would sometimes swim home, while his guest would return by gondola with his clothes. When the tide was coming in, it was not too strenuous a swim for a fit, if plump, man; but, alas, the tom-tom of the English colony would summon the fans to the embankment of the Grand Canal where they watched, rapturously, as he stroked his way home. When he entered the foyer of a Venetian theatre, space would be cleared and a circle of gawkers formed around him. Byron's fourteen servants were also known to accept bribes from English visitors who wanted to see not his study but his bedroom. He moved on to Ravenna; then to romantic death at Missolonghi.

Across the Grand Canal, Richard Wagner worked on his opera, *Tristan and Isolde*, bringing his own piano and his own bed with him from Germany – life was better organised in those days – and he returned to Venice for the last months of *his* life in the Vendramin Palace. During this final visit, he was joined by his father-in-law, Franz Liszt, a genuine pop star at the age of thirteen, the 'Paganini of the ivories'. A handsome, dashing Hungarian, pursued by women, he had briefly interrupted his career to become first, a Franciscan friar, and then an ordained abbè, which may have excited his public all the more.

Love and death were the great themes of the Romantic Age, and they constantly intertwined. George Sand came here with Alfred de Musset. Upon

The gardens of the
Palazzo Cappello, another
palace where Henry James
lived and worked. Not all
patrician palaces in Venice
had gardens and when they
did they were likely to be
sheltered from public view.
The Venetians had other
ways of being ostentacious
in displaying their wealth.

A votive shrine. Love and death were the two themes that permeated nineteenth-century Venice.

RIGHT
Florian's café. Opened in 1720, it became one of Europe's most famous coffee-houses and was open twenty-four hours a day.

arrival he told her, 'George, I do not love you'. So she wrote a novel. George Eliot came here with her young husband. On their first night together, he flung himself out of the bedroom and into the Grand Canal. All in all, Venice has never been a lucky city for women in love, called George.

Happily there were a number of non-practising romantics who stayed out of canals. Near the Accademia Bridge stand two palaces built by the Barbaro family, the same family that built the villa at Maser. One of the Barbaro palaces was bought and restored by an American family in the 1880s. Here the greatest of American novelists, Henry James, came and stayed. It is nice to think of him at my age – and weight – struggling up the palace's lop-sided stairs.

The rooms are still pretty much the way they were when James lived there, and when Browning dropped by to give poetry readings. John Singer Sargent and Claude Monet both worked in the Barbaro rooms, and Henry James used this palace as a setting for *The Wings of the Dove*. 'I have this vast cool upper floor', he wrote, 'all scirocco draughts and easy undressedness quite to myself. These ever adorable (never more so) marble halls.'

When the palace's owner showed me the desk where James wrote *The Aspern Papers*, I expressed some doubts. When she asked me why, I said that I didn't think there was a writer ever born, with the possible exception of Ernest Hemingway, who could write with a mirror in front of him – and his own face reflected. She laughed and showed me a photograph of the way the desk looked when James was here: the Master had ordered the mirrored top section to be removed.

Until this century the gondola was the preferred way of getting about the canals of Venice. Though there are now fewer gondolas and gondoliers than there were in Henry James's day, they still attract tourists who enjoy the way the gondoliers throw themselves, in James's words, 'over the tremendous oar. It [the gondola] has the boldness of a bird and the regularity of a pendulum'. The poet Arthur Henry Clough was thrilled by his gondola, writing:

> *How light we move, how swiftly, ah*
> *Were life but as the gondola.*

To which one might add, if life were like the gondola today, life would be far too expensive to live. On the other hand, the beauty of the gondoliers' voices, raised in song, is, perhaps, beyond price. Wagner was inspired by the gondolier's long drawn-out mournful call when poling home alone, and used it as the shepherd's horn at the beginning of the Third Act of *Tristan and Isolde*. Nowadays, on a moonlit glide in a gondola, you are more likely to hear, sometimes from a tape recording, songs praising Naples, or inviting you to return next time to Sorrento.

The lagoon lit by a winter sunset.

The cemetery on
S. Michele. In its
Orthodox section, the
Russian ballet impresario,
Serge Diaghilev, who died
in Venice in 1929, is
buried in a small
mausoleum. A young
unknown Russian
composer, hired by
Diaghilev, is buried nearby
with a simple stone
marker. His name was
Igor Stravinsky.

On Venice's beautiful island of the dead is an enigmatic memorial which simply bears the name 'Sonia'.

Other visitors in the past found the gondola somewhat too creepily reminiscent of a coffin. And the gondola does indeed suggest a coffin when it becomes a hearse, transporting a body from the city to a special island of the dead, the island of S. Michele. There, space is limited, and unless you are rich or famous, your bones are removed after about twelve years and taken to a more remote common grave on another island. One of the most touching sights is the grave of the great ballet impressario, Diaghilev. A young ballerina has hung her ballet slippers on his simple monument. Ever curious, I examined the shoes and discovered something never before noted: she had two left feet. No Tom Coryate, she.

*A panoramic view of
Venice today, with the
magnificent clock tower of
St. Mark's Square in
the foreground.*

X

THE CITY TODAY

*The unplanned Empire and the carefully calculated Republic
have both faded away. Today, Venice could be called the Empress
of European Tourism. The eighteenth-century Grand Tour,
which would have been incomplete without Venice, may have
little in common with the twentieth-century tourist industry,
but Venice remains the Italian city most difficult to reach
and most worth the trouble.*

VENICE Incorporated is still very much in business. The tourists arrive in
their hundreds of thousands from all over the world. In fact, it seems to
be an integral law of tourism that the smaller the place, the bigger the
crowd. Today there are only 83,000 Venetians residing in historic Venice. The
modern Venetian, though detesting the crowded *vaporetti* and streets as much
as the visitors do, has adapted himself to the situation. 'Venetians are like
aquatic birds, now on sea, now on land', Cassiodorus wrote in the sixth
century. Always bobbing about for a morsel or for prey. Since few of today's
Venetian birds can afford to migrate to equally bountiful climes when winter
comes, their sometimes pelican-like appetite during the warmer months,
when the tourists also are bobbing about on the lagoon, may be explained as
their natural way of storing up enough nourishing funds for the leaner
months. Few are the Venetian families of any class who do not benefit,
directly or indirectly, from the annual invasion of tourists. In fact, many spend
the winter months preening themselves for the onslaught. If they are hotel-
keepers that might take the form of devising ways of turning two single
bedrooms into three.

Survival, and success, began and ended with boats – with rowing, with the
great galleys. Fathers taught sons, generation after generation. The Voga
Longa, or 'Long Row', is not a race so much as a commemoration, a reminder
to Venetians of who they once were – and are. Each spring, all Venetians who
want to take part in the newly-established Voga Longa can do so. The route
round the lagoon and back to the Grand Canal is twenty miles long. Venetians
row standing up so that they can study the water and the treacherous mud.
Venetians, by nature, are watchful.

OVERLEAF
*The basin of St. Mark's,
filled with boats at the
start of the Voga Longa –
a new boating race which
is open to everyone. Five
grey-haired ladies from
Bavaria arrive every year
for the 25-mile race around
Venice's main island. It is
modern Venice's marathon
where the least likely
contenders can win.*

PAGE 143 ABOVE
*These stout-hearted men are
either veterans of the French
navy or cooks, judging by
their costumes.*

PAGE 143 BELOW
*This seems more like a
Bangkok ('the Venice of
the East') floral float than
a racing vehicle.*

Modern-day transport. The motor boat in Venice is usually a water-taxi, and the waves it generates have been blamed for the corrosion of many buildings' foundations.

They also stand up to row because the shallowness of most of the small canals gives them the chance to use their oars as poles. They invented the gondola, with its flat bottom, to allow them to glide along the surface of the water, and to free the boat more easily from mudbanks. Even the *vaporetti* have been designed especially by Venetians for local needs; but they are, of course, no longer propelled by steam (*vapore*), but diesel oil. The American novelist, William Dean Howells, as a young American consul in Venice in the 1860s, said that the first steam-operated public transport boats were called 'omnibuses', so our seemingly silly translation of 'water-bus' for *vaporetto* has a precedent.

Surely the last book to recommend that visitors should see Venice by the traditional means of transport, rather than as a special treat, was published in London as late as 1954. The sentence 'Your gondola passes among these humble folk [on the Giudecca] as in a dream', brings today's reader up with a start, as if the author, Edward Hutton, had suddenly transferred himself backwards into the last century.

There were once more than 10,000 gondolas in Venice, which conjures up the image of frequent traffic jams. By the mid-1600s, the number was reduced to about 8,500, and today there are said to be some 350 gondolas in Venice, though many of those may be in semi-permanent drydock. Once a gondola's oars were handed down from father to son, as the boat's life span was half a century. Now, because of the damage done by the waves of motorboats and water-taxis, a gondola becomes firewood after twenty years. A few years ago, a private German-Italian committee was set up to save the gondola from total extinction. In plain words, this meant subsidising the last remaining gondola shipyard, which is near the S. Trovaso Church. It also meant finding and training young men to build the boats, which is still the Committee's main problem. A fully-fitted gondola, with all accessories, none of them really optional, costs between 12,000 and 15,000 dollars. If one could persuade Arab or Texan oil millionaires that life is but an incomplete dream without a gondola moored by the front porch, the craft might attract more young builders and guarantee the continuous presence of the gondola in the city of its invention.

If any Venetian family still owns a private gondola, it almost certainly does not maintain its own gondolier any longer. (The Cassa di Risparmio, the powerful local Savings Bank, has a splendid gondola, brought out on great occasions, but rowed by a professional gondolier hired for the day.) It now officially costs 50,000 lire to hire a manned gondola for a 50-minute hour, though that is likely to be your starting price; the final fee will be agreed upon when you near the gondolier's own estimate. Divided between four or six passengers, the price is right for a rare experience.

*Next to the Church of S. Trovaso stands the only
gondola shipyard (squero) still in business. Foreign
and Italian groups have banded together to guarantee
its survival. (There was no saint called Trovaso – the
name of the church is an example of the Venetians'
impatient contraction of paired saints, in this case
Gervasio and Protasio, sons of S. Vidal).*

*ABOVE A gondola with
its traditional fittings,
moored in a side canal.*

*LEFT A working barge
delivers goods from the
mainland. The canal, a
thoroughfare both vital and
ornamental, is still the
basis of the life of the city.*

You can also say you have been on a gondola ride by taking one of the gondola ferries, which will pole you across the Grand Canal at six authorised and often essential points. The current charge for the 90-second shuttle, which one Venetian said recently used to be roughly the same as the cost of a pack of cigarettes, is now ridiculously low – 200 lire, or one-tenth the cost of a pack. These ferries are primarily for local use, by countesses, their poodles, and delivery boys. Passengers are expected to stand up, perfectly balanced, during the brief crossing. They are not recommended for vertiginous tourists.

Life goes on, with or without an empire. There are no doges now, there is no fleet, there are no victorious admirals. But there are still Venetian heroes. . . . Like Arrigo Cipriani, hereditary proprietor of the world's most famous bar, Harry's Bar. Cipriani is a new representative of an old tradition, that is to say, he is a highly ingenious creator of what the Venetians still most respect – wealth for their city.

Harry's Bar may be Venice's most successful invention since Venice itself. In 1931, an American lamented with his favourite hotel bartender, the late Giuseppe Cipriani, that what Venice lacked was a good bar. The American, whose name was Harry, probably was not the first refugee from American Prohibition to make that observation, although the lengthy Venetian chronicles of two other Americans, Henry James and William Dean Howells, carry no mention of the city's lack of saloons. But Harry was the first to follow the inbred American tradition of wanting to set right a wrong. This was done in the form of financial backing to Cipriani, who found a rope storeroom next to the St. Mark's *vaporetto* stop and there opened what he called Harry's Bar.

Even without knowing the origin of its history, some American visitors today consider Harry's Bar as being almost extra-territorially *theirs*. Since the closing of the American consulate in the 1970s, it is indeed sometimes the only place for Americans in acute distress to go for comfort and advice. However, Harry's Bar was and remains an entirely Venetian operation, though the babble of barbaric voices on summer days and nights is predominantly American. Most important, it is an innovation, perhaps the only one in the ancient city, which has been accepted by the Venetians. It has become one of their own monuments. Like most natives everywhere, they may shy away from actually visiting their monuments (call it the Grant's Tomb or Tower of London syndrome), but they like to know that it is there, and that it is appreciated and frequented by foreign visitors. The bar and the restaurant are always under the watchful eye of Arrigo (the nearest Italian equivalent of Harry), and when he and his son, Roberto, rowed in the Voga Longa race, they were cheered by the Venetians lining the embankments as local heroes. Nothing succeeds like success, and in Venice nothing succeeds like selling Venice, particularly to satisfied customers.

*Arrigo Cipriani and his
son head the Voga Longa
boatmen as they row down
the Grand Canal. An
artist is painting the scene
from the balcony of the
Palazzo Falier, where the
young American consul,
William Dean Howells,
lived in the 1860s.*

The Peggy Guggenheim
Collection in the Palazzo
Venier dei Leoni is open to
the public, though the iron
water-gate in winter is usually
closed. This is the rear
view of Marini's bronze
Angel of the Citadel,
looking towards the Grand
Canal. The sculpture's
front view is one reason
why the gates are kept
shut.

In summer, three orchestras
play, not simultaneously,
in the three outdoor cafés of
St. Mark's Square. The
music can be quite good,
and should be enjoyed, as a
supplementary charge for
music will be put on your
bill.

LEFT Crowds in
St. Mark's Square create a
kaleidoscope of colour.
Except for the colder
months of the year, this
looks like an average day
for the Square, the only
one in Venice to be called a
'piazza' because even in
name Venetians felt it
should be unique.

Venice is a city of reflections.

The only legal gambling today in Venice is still run by the local government, at the winter casino in the Vendramin Palace and at the summer casino on the Lido. Carnival faded away with the Republic itself; but an attempt to revive it, as a tourist attraction, came in with the new Communist-Socialist city council in the early 1980s. In 1985, they also planned to revive bull-fighting in Campo S. Polo, guaranteeing that it would be bloodless, with imported torreros only 'worrying' the bulls. Meanwhile, until the bulls arrive, as a distraction, they held a 'Miss Courtesan of 1985' contest.

If each Carnival visitor was obliged to take home one Venetian pigeon, the pigeon problem could have been resolved. For pigeon droppings can, and do, corrode marble. The city fathers now plan to import jackdaws (the *corvus monedula*) from Holland, giving them a municipal roost in the eaves of the Frari Church. The jackdaw is a noted thief, with a passion for other birds' nests. It is reckoned that in five years' time, the pigeons will be permanently and 'naturally' evicted by the thieving birds from St. Mark's Square, itself a showcase for stolen treasures from the past. The bailiffs who stand guard outside the church will, doubtless, be warned that the jackdaw reputedly likes to steal gold coins. Otherwise, the final solution to Venice's pigeon problem might well bring an end to the church's gold mosaics, as chip by chip they are spirited away to stolen nests.

Why do people still come to Venice, a city not easy of access and certainly not easy on the tourist's budget? What am I doing in St. Mark's Square when I've never met a pigeon that I liked? What are *they* doing here – all these people? Millions come here every year, and thousands came in past centuries. (And I am improvising, rather desperately, dialogue to a camera in the far distance as pigeons and tourists stare in horror at the man talking loudly to himself.) Well, I have a hunch that most of the people who come here hope to find something that they've never known before. For the visitor it is a sort of waking dream. Naturally, no Venetian ever dreams this Venice, but every Venetian works to evoke it for others.

Water gave birth to Venice. Water protected Venice from enemies. Water made Venice rich, first through the salt trade, then with ships and commerce. Now it is the tourists who make Venice rich, who come to see themselves reflected. Venetian glass is like Venetian water. You are reflected. The reflection is real, but is the thing reflected real? Venetians tend to prefer reflections to the flesh and the mask to either. As the twentieth century draws to a close, no one knows quite what to expect, if anything, of the future. There is a strong need for magic, for a place that is outside of time, for a postponement of reality. For Venice.

*A final view of the city at sunset. A motorboat churns
the waters of the lagoon as it leaves Venice.*

BEHIND THE CAMERA

If you are a tourist in Venice, with a typical good quality camera, the results are likely to be clichéd and transitory. That is not to say that these clichés are not stunning. This is the nature of Venice.

The true flavour is only discovered after several visits, when the labyrinth of *calle* and canals is no longer a mystery and you can feel at ease on your wanderings and avoid the crushing main through-routes. The changing light also becomes apparent with time, and only if you were to live there as a photographer, would you have the opportunity to record all the moods created by the light and shade. It is to be hoped that during my four visits a different light has shone upon the inevitable clichés in this book, but it seems no work on Venice is complete without them.

The challenge to obtain good photographs faced with batteries of tourist cameras going off all around you, requires calm philosophy – and a better camera. The equipment must give you the biggest picture size with the best optics that you can carry and use freely. Pentax 6 cm × 7 cm is the format giving studio quality transparencies out of a soft bag. The freedom this can give you helps predict the importance of the subject before you. Anticipation of time, and its length, is the key element in a photograph and it requires patient determination in Venice – the calm philosophy.

I have photographed many subjects more than once, revisiting them often while I'm there and at various times of the day and night. Working at night is always exciting; otherwise I wouldn't have seen *Carnevale*, the *acqua alta*, or just the magic of Venice after dark.

Local knowledge is essential when working overseas and without the help of Guido Salsilli and Gorgo the Boatman, life would have been more of a slog and much less fun. Their help contributed towards my efforts to do Venice justice. Not a contrived attraction, but a living fairy tale.

Tore Gill

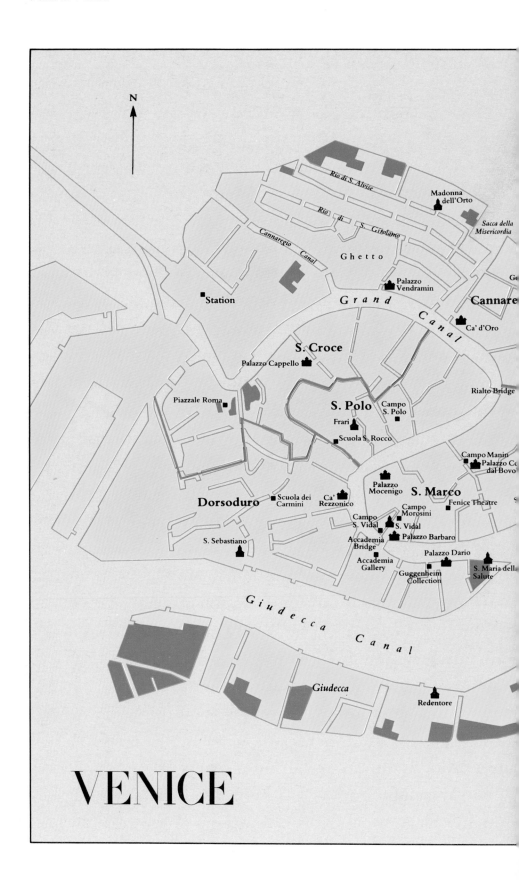

N

Rio di S. Alvise

Madonna
dell'Orto

Rio   di   S. Girolamo

Sacca della
Misericordia

Cannaregio Canal

Ghetto

Station

Palazzo
Vendramin

G

Grand   *Canal*

Cannare

Ca' d'Oro

S. Croce

Palazzo Cappello

Piazzale Roma

Rialto Bridge

S. Polo

Campo
S. Polo

Frari

Scuola S. Rocco

Campo Manin

Palazzo C
dal Bovo

Palazzo
Mocenigo

S. Marco

Dorsoduro

Scuola dei
Carmini

Ca'
Rezzonico

Campo
Morosini

Fenice Theatre

Campo
S. Vidal

S. Vidal

Accademia
Bridge

Palazzo Barbaro

S. Sebastiano

Accademia
Gallery

Palazzo Dario

Guggenheim
Collection

S. Maria della
Salute

Giudecca   Canal

Giudecca

Redentore

VENICE

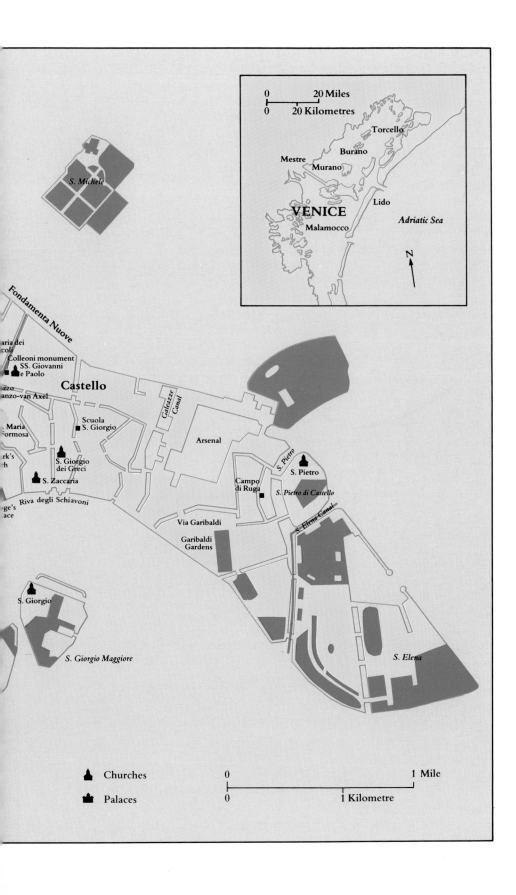

0   20 Miles
0   20 Kilometres

Torcello
Burano
Mestre
Murano
VENICE
Lido
Adriatic Sea
Malamocco

N

S. Michele

Fondamenta Nuove
aria dei
coli
Colleoni monument
SS. Giovanni
e Paolo
Castello
azzo
anzo-van Axel
Scuola
S. Giorgio
Maria
Formosa
Galeazze Canal
Arsenal
S. Pietro
rk's
h
S. Giorgio
dei Greci
Campo
di Ruga
S. Pietro
S. Zaccaria
S. Pietro di Castello
ge's
ace
Riva degli Schiavoni
Via Garibaldi
S. Elena Canal
Garibaldi
Gardens
S. Giorgio
S. Giorgio Maggiore
S. Elena

▲ Churches
🏛 Palaces

0   1 Mile
0   1 Kilometre

SELECTED BIBLIOGRAPHY

Bull, George, *Venice, The Most Triumphant City*,
THE FOLIO SOCIETY, London, 1960

Coryat, Thomas, *Coryat's Crudities*, 2 volumes,
JAMES MACLEHOSE AND SONS, Glasgow, 1905

Frigeni, Mariana, *Il Condottiero*,
LONGANESI, Milan, 1985

Hale, John R., 'Quattrocento Venice'
in *Cities of Destiny*, Arnold Toynbee (ed.),
London, 1967

Honour, Hugh, *The Companion Guide to Venice*,
COLLINS, London, 1965

Lane, Frederick C., *Venice: A Maritime Republic*,
JOHNS HOPKINS UNIVERSITY PRESS, Baltimore, 1973

Lauritzen, Peter, and Zielcke, Alexander, *Palaces of Venice*,
PHAIDON, Oxford, 1978

Lorenzetti, Giulio, *Venice and Its Lagoon*,
EDIZIONI LINT, Trieste, 1975

Lutyens, Mary (ed.), *Effie in Venice*,
JOHN MURRAY, London, 1965

McAndrew, John, *Venetian Architecture of the Early Renaissance*,
MIT, Cambridge, Mass., 1980

McCarthy, Mary, *Venice Observed*,
WILLIAM HEINEMANN, London, 1961

Morris, James, *Venice*,
FABER AND FABER, London, 1960

Norwich, John Julius, *History of Venice*,
VIKING, 1982

Pullan, Brian (ed.), *Crisis and Change in the Venetian Economy*,
METHUEN, London, 1968

Pullan, Brian, *Rich and Poor in Renaissance Venice*,
OXFORD, 1971

Rendina, Claudio, *I Dogi*,
NEWTON COMPTON EDITORI, Rome, 1984

Tenenti, Alberto, *Piracy and the Decline of Venice, 1580–1615*,
LONGMANS, GREEN AND CO. LTD, London, 1967

PHOTOGRAPHIC ACKNOWLEDGMENTS

The photographs in this book were all specially taken
for VIDAL IN VENICE by Tore Gill, with the exception
of those listed below, which are reproduced by kind
permission of the following:

Cameraphoto, Venice: 34

Correr Museum, Venice: 24–5, 85

Dover, Michael: *copyright page*

National Gallery, London, the Trustees of: 71, 81, 97 *below*, 116, 125

Querini Stampalia Gallery, Venice: 49, 58 *above* and *below*, 59, 62–3

Ruskin Gallery, Sheffield
(Guild of St. George Collection): 30–31

Scala, Florence: 27, 45, 95, 97 *above*, 98, 99 (Accademia Gallery, Venice), 46, 83 (Vatican Map Library), 94 (S. Giorgio degli Schiavoni), 105 (Correr Museum), 124 (Private Collection)

Scorer, Mischa: 10, 35

The map of Venice was produced by Swanston Graphics, Derby, England

159

INDEX